Mountain Rain

Eileen Crossman

to Douglas

OMF BOOKS

© OVERSEAS MISSIONARY FELLOWSHIP
(formerly China Inland Mission)
Published by Overseas Missionary Fellowship (IHQ) Ltd.,
2 Cluny Road, Singapore 1025,
Republic of Singapore

First published 1982
Reprinted 1984, 1985, 1987
Reprinted 1989

OMF BOOKS are distributed by
OMF, 404 South Church Street, Robesonia, PA 19551, USA
OMF, Belmont, The Vine, Sevenoaks, Kent, TN13 3TZ, UK
OMF, P O Box 849, Epping, NSW 2121, Australia
OMF, 1058 Avenue Road, Toronto, Ontario M5N 2C6, Canada
OMF, P O Box 10159 Balmoral, Auckland, New Zealand
OMF, P O Box 41, Kenilworth 7745, South Africa
and other OMF offices.

ISBN 9971-972-05-0

Printed in Singapore
SW 7K/12/89

ACKNOWLEDGEMENTS

I am indebted to several friends who helped bring about this book: to Dorothy Burrows for laborious research into CIM archives; to Allyn Cooke for lengthy missives sent from Oregon, USA; to Dan Smith for his books sent from Canada; to Leslie Lyall for information on Shansi; to Charles Stammers for advice; to Barbara Collins for so willingly typing the manuscript. It will be clear to readers of *Behind the Ranges* that I am much indebted to Mrs Howard Taylor who first told the story.

I wish also to thank the Overseas Missionary Fellowship — who first approached me about this book — for affording me a new acquaintance with a father whom I scarcely knew, and for bringing back to me those sunny mountains where I lived a long time ago.

Eileen Crossman
Bath, 1982

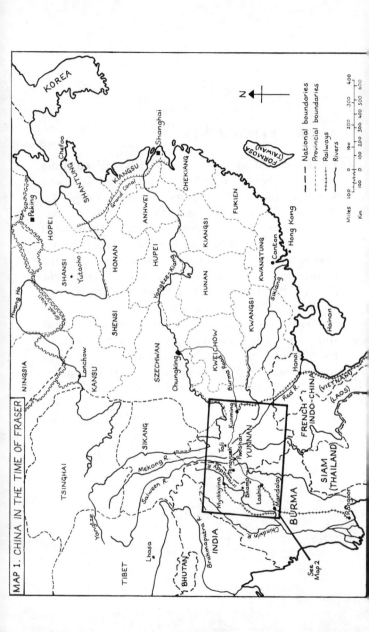

MAP 1. CHINA IN THE TIME OF FRASER

N

National boundaries
Provincial boundaries
Railways
Rivers

Miles 100 0 100 200 300 400
Km 100 0 100 200 300 400 500 600

KOREA

SHANTUNG   Chefoo
■ Peking
HOPEI   Grand Canal   Shanghai ■
SHANSI   Yutaoho   Hwang Ho   KIANGSU
Great Wall   ANHWEI   CHEKIANG
HONAN
NINGSIA   SHENSI   HUPEI   KIANGSI   FUKIEN
KANSU   Lanchow   Yangtze Kiang
HUNAN
FORMOSA (TAIWAN)
TSINGHAI   SZECHWAN   Chungking   KWEICHOW   KWANGSI   KWANGTUNG   Canton   Hong Kong
Burma Road   Sikiang
Yangtze   Mekong R.   Hanoi   Red R.   Hainan
SIKANG   Tali   Kunming
Lhasa   Salween R.   Tengyueh   Paoshan   YUNNAN   FRENCH INDO-CHINA   (VIETNAM)   (LAOS)
TIBET   Myitkyina   Bhamo   Lashio
BHUTAN   Brahmaputra R.   Irrawaddy R.   Mandalay   BURMA   SIAM (THAILAND)
INDIA   Chindwin R.   Rangoon
See Map 2

CONTENTS

FOREWORD

In my student days 'Fraser of Lisuland' was already something of a legend. The spiritual effect in remote tribal areas of small supporting prayer groups in England was giving fresh vision to missionary-minded Christians. *Behind the Ranges,* published in 1944, spread the vision. Now the story is told afresh by one of his daughters.

James Fraser had a great capacity to enjoy life. Friends and relations enjoyed his keen sense of humour. He was also an outstanding pianist, giving his first piano recital in London at the age of twenty. Converted as a student at Imperial College, he was in China by the age of 22, leaving his comfortable wealthy home and the prospect of a brilliant career in engineering. Instead, he chose a life of physical hardship in the rugged mountains of South West China and spiritual conflict among the people of the Lisu tribe who were steeped in centuries of demon worship, and none of whom had ever heard of Jesus Christ.

Battling with bouts of loneliness and fever and sometimes of depression, his encounters with the powers of darkness only increased his confidence in God and in the power of prayer. Eventually, after much heartache and disappointment, believers could be numbered in thousands and churches began to spring up as Lisu Christians spread the gospel among their own people.

This book describes the spiritual battles which accompanied the preaching of the Word of God in a part of the world where idolatry had a total hold on every part of life, and where all disease and disaster was attributed to spirits who must be appeased at all costs. The same principles apply, however, anywhere in the world where the preaching of the gospel is opposed by the entrenched forces of darkness in whatever guise these may appear. We have the same Enemy, but also the same God.

Leith Samuel
Southampton

1 THE WATERSHED

Flight from the Hunter

James saw the flash of a sword before he heard the hunter's curses. The dogs sounded far off now, but the angry Kachin tribesman was leaping down the slope towards him. James turned and slid down a smooth boulder towards the shrivelled pines, glancing over his shoulder at the flying figure behind.

A cascade of loose earth and pebbles passed him as the hunter hurled himself over the boulder. The sword sliced through the air with the sound of a whip.

James's mouth felt dry, and his stomach knotted itself up in his throat. He leapt past the meagre pines and out on the open mountain-side. There was no protection now. It was a race for his life. His sandals slipped and grated on the uneven stones and he felt the thump of his heart fiercely thrusting him on.

The bare feet of the hunter made a small sound behind. The curses had died to a steady breathing as the Kachin closed in on him.

At least, James thought hazily, it's a quick death. With a jerk of his shoulders he dropped his rucksack. His sweat felt cold as he glanced over his shoulder.

The dark head of the hunter bent for a second over the bag. The contents were shaken out and white paper caught the wind. But the Kachin was up and streaking after his quarry, splashing through the slippery stream and up a rising slope into the shadows of brush and oaks.

James was dimly aware of the dark summits of the Burmese mountains ahead, huge and motionless, as the ground flew by beneath him. If it was a question of endurance, he thought, the Kachin would win: he could run for days on end. *His* best friend would be darkness: he must run on until the sudden fall of an eastern night. He began to pray, rather brokenly, as he ran on. 'Whether by life or death . . .' he thought, his mind in a mist.

The hunter's footsteps were almost silent now, but steady and persistent. James sensed somehow that his longer legs were gaining him distance, and fear had lent him incredible speed.

He had been running for over an hour when he heard the barking of dogs again. A Lisu village. His pace eased slightly and he peered through the failing light for the straw roofs. Splashing through the green mud he hurdled the broken boundary fence and slowed down to look back at his pursuer.

The trail was empty.

The evening lit up the opposing hillside, picking out a dark figure steadily moving back up the mountain to the wild and inhospitable regions of the Kachin.

James sat down on the ground and laid his head against the bamboo upright of the fence. His heart was pounding and his head swimming. Suddenly he was engulfed in a deathly weariness. For nearly an hour he lay wrapped in darkness, half awake and half asleep.

He had been captured by bandits before. They had surrounded him, seized him and stripped him. But they had spared his life. He had nearly drowned when he sank in quicksands up to his neck on a journey in

West Yunnan. He had often been shot at by armed
men, and as for thieves and burglars by night — they
had become just a mild inconvenience. But this cross-
country run had really shaken him. There was no
doubt that the Kachin meant to kill.

'He shall deliver thee in six troubles: yea in seven
there shall no evil touch thee' (Job 5.19).

After all, James thought, a Christian is immortal
till his work is done. All the same, he had not expected
such a hostile reaction to his message about Jesus
Christ.

But a lot of unexpected things had happened since
he had arrived in South West China. Not just the
adventures a traveller might meet with anyway. The
most unexpected things had been in the way of
spiritual secrets: the opening up of mysteries he had
thought belonged to heaven. He had little realized
how deeply a man could drink of the cup of fellowship with God down here.

His mind went back over the years to a small scrap
of paper. It seemed a long time ago . . .

A Booklet for a Student
No one was aware of the battle royal taking place in
the heart of the young man sitting in the corner of the
library. For the third time that afternoon he unfolded
the leaflet lying beside his papers and read it through.
A fellow-student had given it to him two days before, when they had been experimenting with steam-
pressure. A conversation had developed between them,
and the leaflet was produced. The young man now sat
bowed over his books, aware only of the intensifying
conflict inside him.

The year was 1906, and the student, James Fraser,

was reading engineering at Imperial College, London. He knew that his field of study held immense prospects worldwide, and he knew that his own ability was considerable. But the twopenny pamphlet struck at the very roots of his assumptions. Always one to question things himself, he now found himself faced with some questions he couldn't comfortably answer.

He had always assumed that he should work hard, develop his gifts, and enter a useful career. Of course, being God-fearing, he should live a moral life and attend church. What more could God ask?

James had done well in mathematics and distinguished himself already in engineering. More than this, he had spent years of practice in music and was soon to give his first London piano recital. A young man of twenty could hardly have achieved more. But the booklet suggested that God was asking for something far and away beyond all this.

James picked up his books and made his way out of the college. Crossing from Kensington to Hyde Park, he eventually reached King's Cross and the early evening train to Letchworth, in Hertfordshire. For two days his mind had been in turmoil and he now found the journey a good deal shortened by the concentration of his thinking. The words of the booklet were very plain, down-to-earth and compelling. Its thought was perfectly cool and logical.

> If our Master returned today to find millions of people unevangelized, and looked, as of course He would look, to us for an explanation, I cannot imagine what explanation we should have to give.
>
> Of one thing I am certain — that most of the excuses we are accustomed to make with such good conscience *now*, we shall be wholly ashamed of *then*.

He stared out of the train windows as the soft fields of Hertfordshire rushed past. A strange excitement seemed to have entered into it all. In momentous decisions in life there is a beckoning joy in God's gateways. The booklet spoke of losing one's life for Christ's sake; of dying in order to live. In short, it spoke of renouncing obvious plans and prospects because God had something better. Better plans, better prospects.

He was thinking hard as he walked along the roads of Letchworth Garden City to Willian Way: a rugged figure, tall, tousled and rather carelessly dressed. His features certainly weren't handsome, though some-how they suggested energy and purpose.

Broken Home

His mother's house was large, though not as large as the big, double-fronted house in St Albans the family had lived in years before, when their parents were still together. James's was a broken home. His parents had separated on grounds of incompatibility during his adolescence.

His mother was the essence of Victorian gentility, immaculate in lace and velvet. She was sensitive to music and art and very alive to things spiritual. His father was a Scots-Canadian, and a highly successful veterinary surgeon. In his earlier years he had practised in the Herriot-famed Yorkshire dales. Later he moved south to St Albans, and for twenty years was President of the Royal College of Veterinary Surgeons. He was also an able public speaker, nominated for Parliament several times, though he didn't stand. He was impatient with trivia and small-mindedness, but he was a staunch Methodist and in later years turned more and more to the Bible. 'Every word of it is true, you know', he wrote to his daughter.

When their differences of temperament became unbearable, Mrs Fraser used her own fortune to buy a house in Letchworth and take her five children with her. From many points of view, things were happier then, though such a move obviously left anguish in its wake.

There was plenty of lively debate in the new home as years went by. One member was in the vanguard of left-wing politics at Cambridge and later joined the Communist party. Some of the family stayed loyal to their father. And now James's new lifestyle was to be misunderstood, which was hardly surprising.

But it wasn't misunderstood by his mother. A spiritual friendship grew up between them which was to last his lifetime. Both had been church-going Methodists, but it wasn't until his student days that James came face to face with Jesus Christ. Even his mother didn't fully appreciate what had happened. For James it was an experience like John Wesley's at Aldersgate Street: his heart was 'strangely warmed' and, for the first time, he fully understood 'the change which God works in the heart through faith in Christ.'

Student Influences
The pamphlet he had been given and the influence of the little Bible studies at Imperial College brought James into a new spiritual country. He always looked on it as his conversion, though some said he seemed a mature Christian straight away.

James was liked by his fellow students at Imperial College. He had an uproarious sense of humour for one thing, and he loved company. His cousin, Alec

Bourne, later the famous surgeon in the 1938 Abortion Case, remembered many holidays spent travelling Europe with him. It was not just the adventures shared and scenery enjoyed that impressed Alec, but James's capacity to enjoy life. *Everything* seemed to interest him. He had a keen sense of the absurd, which enlivened their escapades.

'To think', said his brother Gordon after James's death in 1938, 'we shall never hear that laugh again!'

Another contemporary wryly commented, 'I used to wonder sometimes whether he knew the whole of Alice in Wonderland by heart.'

But James had a serious side, even before his conversion. The difficult and forbidding seemed to appeal to him. He had a dogged perseverence in seeing a job through. As a boy he once cycled 199 miles without getting off his bike. He seemed to enjoy the test of endurance.

But now a whole new dimension of life opened up. God had met with him. A new strong desire laid hold of his mind: 'God who works in me mightily'. He lost interest in the things that had absorbed him before and began to streamline his life like an athlete for the Olympics.

Certainly there weren't any half-measures. There was only one thing that mattered any more. There is no record of his feeling he had renounced anything: he had quite simply found earlier loves eclipsed by a new passion. 'If anyone loves the world, the love of the Father is not in him' (1 John 2.15).

Music
There had to be a pruning, however. He was a powerful pianist, with real size and scope to his

performances. Many years later he wrote a little about
his musical dreams.

> When I dip into real music, I often have the feel-
> ing that a part of myself has been more or less un-
> developed — I do not mean in regard to execution,
> but in regard to general musical education and soul-
> culture. Not that I would have my life different in
> actual practice, if I had the choice of making it so.
> One has sometimes to prune a tree in one direction,
> that it may develop better in another. But if I ever
> dream, and I do sometimes, of golden ages and
> existences, the golden age to me is that of a century
> ago more or less, and the golden existence the swim of
> the musical world in Continental conservatoires. I
> dream of bathing my soul in the creations of
> Beethoven, Mozart and other great masters; of drink-
> ing in opera-music, of living in the world of the
> Rubensteins, Sarasates, Paganinis, and the great
> singers. I know very well that all this never is, nor can
> be wholly satisfying, and I deliberately relegate it to its
> own place. It is not and I do not wish it should be
> more to me than dreams. My natural longings, how-
> ever, go out in that direction.

The same human cost must have been felt about his
engineering prospects and his maths. When he was
later asked if he missed his piano in China, he said
that in many ways he missed his maths books even
more. His mind was vigorous, penetrating and argu-
mentative and naturally enjoyed the subject. But great
and good as these things were, they paled beside his
love for Jesus Christ.

Mission
The great spiritual revival of the mid-nineteenth
century made a profound impact on Christianity in

Britain. In his book *The Second Evangelical Awakening* Dr Orr estimates that at least a million people were added to the churches. Across the Atlantic the influence of the movement was extensive too, and Christians in both Britain and America began to think globally. For centuries, they now realized, the command of Christ to preach worldwide had been virtually ignored. Many societies were formed to send volunteers overseas to unevangelized countries.

The Keswick movement for the deepening of spiritual life among Christians found its message unfailingly resulted in the same concern. The 1904 revival in Wales added momentum to the missionary movement, and the new-style evangelistic campaigns of Moody, Torrey and others also laid emphasis on the worldwide need of evangelism.

The new concern for Mission had all the hallmarks of the Holy Spirit. It was a deep, abiding and passionate concern for the lost. James heard the great preachers of the day, learnt of Hudson Taylor's venture into inland China and met C T Studd at a Christian Training Camp in 1906. By nature thoughtful and reflective, he was not carried away by passing enthusiasms. But he was so mastered by God in these student days, and so total in his commitment, that he made spiritual strides to a place far beyond his years.

The most valuable of all lessons James learned in these formative years was discipline.

Much as he enjoyed the crowded meetings and the warmth of fellowship, he learnt early to cultivate a personal communion with God. His mother noted that he spent a good deal of time alone in prayer and study of the Bible as a student, 'even though he did not talk much about it.' His studies were systematic and

careful; always with a practical emphasis. Academic
theology was less interesting to him than Christian
dynamics.

Application Forms for China

After taking his degree, James applied to the China
Inland Mission. Everything about this society
answered a chord in his heart. For one thing they
never asked anyone for money; nor even seemed to
mention it. No collections, no appeals, no needs
advertized, and yet within forty years they were
supporting over a thousand members. The general
director and the newest recruit had equal allowances.
All their needs had been supplied. 'God means just
what He says', said Hudson Taylor, 'and He will do
all that He has promised.'

For another thing the mission was inter-denomi-
national. The basis of faith was unequivocally biblical,
but differences on secondary things were not divisive.
There was overriding unity in matters of faith and
doctrine and in the great commission, 'Go ye into all
the world and preach the gospel.'

The CIM was a fairly new mission, and not at all
respectable. 'If James must be absurd', said a member
of his family with some asperity, 'can't he go with a
decent Church Society — some Board Mission? Must
he go with this peculiar bunch?'

But to this peculiar bunch he applied.

It is clear now, with the perspective of a little
distance, that God was undoubtedly with them. In the
annals of church history there are few stories of greater
faith and courage than that of Hudson Taylor's
advance into the interior of China. For the thrills of an
adventure story it makes compelling reading. But the
really moving experience is in tracing the hand of

a gracious and compassionate God in sending messengers, through suffering and bloodshed, to bring the light of knowledge of Him to a quarter of the world's population.

As a matter of fact, James was twice rejected. He had a minor ear infection which the mission feared might worsen in primitive inland China. Better no missionary, however great the need, than one God has not sent, they said; and He only sends those in good health to China.

'Well I'm going there anyway,' James wrote to them at the third attempt, 'because I know I've been sent by God.'

The ear infection cleared; he was accepted. At 21 he began his year's training at the CIM headquarters in North London.

Although he had been to boarding school and University James now began to live with all sorts and temperaments of people at much closer quarters. He took naturally to the fairly spartan life style (even pretending he had to live like this on his visits home). But here, at the long tables of the training home, he got down to Bible study in a new way. It is impressive to see how clear a grasp he had of all the major fundamental doctrines, and how wide and detailed was his knowledge of the Bible even as a young man of 22.

It was always interesting to meet missionaries coming and going at headquarters. They seemed such everyday people, many doing very ordinary jobs so inconspicuously. But they had plenty of stories to tell, and it was inspiring to hear them pray. He grew in understanding and deepened in commitment during the daily prayer-meetings.

These people, he said later, seemed to be filled with the knowledge of God's will in all wisdom and spiritual understanding.

It was a bitter parting for his mother when his year's training was up. James had so much to look forward to. She had only the void of his absence — this son who had brought so much richness into her rather tragic life. Staring out into the darkened garden the night before he left, she realized that it might be ten years or more before she would speak to him. Letters would take months to arrive. How could she pray for him in such a vacuum?

The send-off of missionaries from Victoria station in London was quite different from anything seen in the jet age. Crowds of well-wishers were on the platform. The sound of singing half-drowned the noise of engines and shouts of porters. Reserved and quiet Mrs Fraser and James's sister Millicent stood at the back of the crowd. Neither James nor his mother knew many of the people on the platform. They did not know who had started the singing. But they did know a little, as the train drew out, of what it meant to die.

2   MONKEY PEOPLE

Two Kinds of Mountain

You need to look at the map at the end of this book to understand the terrain of South-West China and why God chose a mountaineer to send there. The Burma road had not been built when James first rode on horseback into Yunnan. To the north-west range upon range of mountains, rising to 19,000 feet, stretched away to the foothills of the Himalayas; wild and forbidding country leading to the borders of Tibet. The mountains of the south-west led over high passes into the lush valleys of Burma.

James was no mean writer in describing a mountain journey.

> Long grass, enormous boulders, rocks of every size, streams and high mountains were all that was to be seen anywhere . . . and the mist rolled in upon us in drizzling rain. We only met one man all day, for the upper slopes afford food and shelter to none but leopards, wolves and bears. This lofty, scrubby, rocky, wet, wild country — how I just revel in it!
>
> But the mist which hid everything below hid all above and around us too. Peak and plain were alike invisible. And the grand, soul-stirring *silence* of these mountains! After our arduous climb, hour after hour (myself just in my element and perfectly happy!) we reached the summit, or rather the pass, for of course no mountain road ever goes over a peak. It was a wood — silent but for our footsteps on the wet, rotten

leaves, and the occasional spat, spat, of big drops of
water falling on the soft spongy ground. Wet, silent,
lonely — not even the call of a bird — it must have
been some ten thousand feet high: and most of the
year covered with snow.

Then came the steep descent on the further side,
hands and feet alike in use as we clambered over mossy
tree-trunks and through brushwood. For a long way,
nothing was to be seen above or below the mist. Then
suddenly (you only look up at intervals when
negotiating such a path), my breath was almost taken
away by seeing all the mountains of Tien-tan and
beyond, as well as the plain far down below, clearly
outspread before me. Such a magnificent view, wide
and sweeping, made me pause awhile to take it in —
range upon range of dark mountains, swathed in
cloud, and in the far distance the forbidding mass of
the Salween Divide, barring the way like a solid wall.
Down, down, down, every now and again stopping to
take in the grandeur of the scene, until almost sun-
down, when we reached the Lisu village of Shui Chen,
wet, bedraggled and weary.

James had arrived in South-West China because
veteran John McCarthy refused to give up on the
province. The CIM directors really felt they should
leave this hinterland for evangelizing at a later date.
They were short of workers as it was, for a country so
vast and a population of nearly 700 million (in-
cidentally at the time of writing over 1,000 million).
However, McCarthy felt so strongly about it that they
told him to visit the Language School where the new
recruits were — James among them — and secretly
select one or two who might be right for the job.

McCarthy sent HQ a telegram after his visit. 'Send
Fraser and anyone else you like.'

So it was that short, stout John McCarthy and tall, lean James Fraser rode up through Burma and over the mountains into Yunnan. The mules were sure-footed on the trails and James and his friend read Chinese newspapers or books as they jogged along. James developed a habit of propping up the score of a Mozart overture or Chopin prelude and 'enjoying the music' as he rode. No cassettes to hand in those days.

They had a few mishaps even on this first journey. Hearing the hooves of his companion's mount behind him one morning, James asked McCarthy's opinion of a book he was reading. The answer seemed a long time coming. Turning round, he found McCarthy's saddle empty, his mule nonchalantly coming along without him. Miles back on the trail, he found McCarthy lying dazed from his fall. No bones appeared to be broken. The old veteran soon staggered to his feet and was back in the saddle.

James's first home was in a town called Tengyueh in the far west, looking up at the mountains of the Burma border. It was a populous area, but many days' journey away from any other missionaries. His home was a little rented room, twelve foot by fourteen, over a Chinese inn. It was bare, but had fewer rats than that of his fellow workers, Mr and Mrs Embery. Here James sat for most of the day studying the Chinese language. Although he had spent six months in the Language School before coming to Tengyueh, the task of mastering Chinese seemed mountainous.

This mountain is called The Chinese Language. It is very steep at first, but gradually seems easier as you go up. Then, just when you feel you are getting on, another peak comes into view, rising up higher than the first, but all part of the same mountain. This also

has to be climbed. It is called Chinese Thought and
Modes of Expression. You had been told all about it
before you began to scramble up the first mountain
but you did not see it then. And the first glimpse
shows how far it is above you.

He had some dispiriting moments when, after days
of study, he would come into the bustling market
place to try out some phrases and find no-one understood a word.

> I am trying my best (he wrote) to get hold of a good
> colloquial knowledge of Chinese, but it will take a
> long time — I am only at the beginning yet. This is
> more important, I feel, than to become a learned
> Chinese scholar, for after all the chief thing is to talk
> in a way easy to be understood. Mr McCarthy told us
> of a missionary, years ago, who was extraordinarily
> accomplished as a Chinese scholar, but whose own
> servant could not understand him in everyday matters!
> There certainly is something fascinating about the
> study of literary Chinese — which must go hand in
> hand with work on the colloquial — but I imagine it
> would be easy to be too much taken up with it.

He jotted down some phrases he overheard in the
inn or the marketplace and tried to rehearse them back
in his room.

> I have taken down several hundred phrases in this
> way. The temptation is to be content to use words
> which nearly express your meaning, but not quite . . .
> For instance you learn the Chinese for 'this is badly
> done', and might make it do duty for clothes not
> washed clean, a room not properly tidied up, a picture
> not hung straight, a piece of meat half-cooked, a
> matter unsatisfactorily settled, etc., etc. But the
> Chinese make distinctions in these things, as we do in
> English.

Temptations

Alone in his attic room James was assailed by some
real temptations. One was a depressing sense of
loneliness in his isolated position. There was virtually
no-one to talk to, since Embery was more than busy in
the work almost single-handed, and James could not
converse in Chinese. Another was the boredom of his
daily study-routine, partly done with his language
teacher, partly alone with his books. Overall there was
the temptation to slacken in his daily communion
with God, that 'secret history of the affection of the
soul.'

Discipline again became all-important to him in
maintaining his walk with God. He had to get up
early, before the inn grew lively and distracting. He
soon found 'prayer-haunts' in places on the hills,
different ones for different weather. A habit formed
early was to walk up and down, praying aloud,
talking as a man talks to his friend. He often used a
hymn-book, praying aloud the words of the hymns.
Sometimes he would pray for the city as he sat and
looked over it from the hills.

James was only 22, and fast learning to school
himself against the subtle inroads of apathy and
lethargy. He tried hard to be faithful in the seemingly
trivial tasks at hand.

'A little thing' said Hudson Taylor, 'is a little thing.
But faithfulness in a little thing is a great thing.'

James wrote at this time:

> It has come home to me very forcibly of late that it
> matters little what the work is in which we are
> engaged: so long as God has put it into our hands, the
> faithful doing of it is of no greater importance in one
> case than in another . . . The temptation I have often

had to contend with is persistent under many forms:
'If only I were in such and such a position' for
example, 'shouldn't I be able to do a great work! Yes, I
am only studying engineering at present, but when I
am in training for missionary work things will be
different and more helpful.' Or 'I am just in preparation at present, taking Bible courses and so on,
but when I get out to China my work will begin.' 'Yes,
I have left home now, but I am only on the voyage,
you know; when I am really in China, I shall have a
splendid chance of service.' Or, 'Well, here in the
Training Home, all my time must be given to language study — how can I do missionary work? But
when I am settled down in my station and able to
speak freely, opportunities will be unlimited!' etc., etc.

It is all IF and WHEN. I believe the devil is fond of
those conjunctions . . . I have to-day, to a limited
extent, the opportunities to which he has been putting
me off (not that I have always yielded to these
temptations), but far from helping me to be faithful in
the use of them, he now turns quite a different face.
The plain truth is that the Scriptures never teach us to
wait for opportunities of service, but to serve in just
the things that lie next to our hands . . . The Lord bids
us work, watch and pray; but Satan suggests, wait
until a good opportunity for working, watching and
praying presents itself — and needless to say, this
opportunity is always in the future . . . Since the
things that lie in our immediate path have been
ordered of God, who shall say that one kind of work is
more important and sacred than another? I believe it is
no more necessary to be faithful (one says it reverently)
in preaching the Gospel than in washing up dishes in
the scullery. I am no more doing the Lord's work in
giving the Word of God to the Chinese than you are,
for example, in wrapping up a parcel to send to the
tailor. It is not for us, in any case, to choose our work.

And if God has chosen it for us, hadn't we better go straight ahead and do it, without waiting for anything greater, better or 'nobler'?

And so, in these early days, James sorted out his tenses. There is no such thing as spiritual victory if it is not in the present tense.

We often say, 'I am looking forward to this, that or the other. Have we any right to be so dissatisfied with our present condition, which God has ordained for us, that we hanker after something in the future? I can hardly see that we have. There is one great exception — we are to look forward with earnest expectation to the coming of the Lord. But we have to be patient even in this. And to look for our Saviour's appearing is a very different thing from hankering after enjoyments of which we hope to partake some time ahead . . . Why should I, in the hot, close, rainy season at Tengyueh, long for the dry months when things are more pleasant all round? Didn't God intend me to put up with the discomfort of heat and mildew? Why should I look forward to the time when I shall be able to speak Chinese more freely? Didn't God intend me to serve an apprenticeship in learning the language? Why should I look forward to a little more time for myself, for reading, etc.? Though it is the most natural thing in the world to have such thoughts, I feel they are not at all scriptural. There is more of the flesh about them than the spirit. And they seem to be inconsistent with the peace of God which, it is promised, shall guard our hearts and our thoughts through Jesus Christ . . . The apostle Paul said that he had 'learned', in whatsoever state he was, 'therein to be content', implying that he had reached that attitude through discipline. And I suppose it must be so with all of us; the natural tendency is to be always straining after something in the future.

James's first halting attempts at preaching brought encouragement from Embery. Although he was now able to speak a little on the streets, he had not previously had to address a group, and when the first assignment to preach in the chapel came he was very nervous. He spent a long time preparing notes for this. What exactly has a missionary come to say?

In preparing my address, I first went through the Acts of the Apostles and some other passages, comparing them with a view to finding out the actual Gospel we are bidden to preach . . . The result was very instructive to me. I had never imagined the Gospel was so simple. Why, Peter and Paul both preached the Gospel in words which would not take one minute to say!

And I found out that there are just four things which seem to be essential in preaching the Gospel.

1   The crucifixion of Jesus Christ — no theological explanation needed.

2   The resurrection of Jesus Christ — most important of all. The Gospel was never preached without this being brought in.

3   Exhortation to hearers to repent of their sins.

4   Promise to all who believe on Jesus Christ that they will receive remission of their sins.

Beyond these four points others are mentioned occasionally, but they are not many . . . In teaching Christians, it is quite another matter. To them we are to declare 'the whole counsel of God', as far as they can receive it. But the Gospel as preached to the unsaved is as simple as it could be. I should not care to take the responsibility of preaching 'another Gospel'.

The first exercise seemed well enough received for him to start out in the market-place explaining to the people the basic truths of the faith. To consolidate the message, he gave out leaflets to those who could read.

First Glimpse of the Tribesmen

The market place at Tengyueh was a hive of activity. With all the Chinese flair for business, traders would bustle in from all parts of the south-west with vegetables, household goods, strange medicines and curious ornaments, setting up open stalls or squatting on the earth, haggling over fractions of a penny and jostling for position and profits. Groups of travellers could be seen at all hours of the day, trudging dust-weary along the grey roads and past the earthen houses. There were the animals too. Pigs and chickens asserted their rights over rotting refuse among the beggars. Overladen mules with bleeding backs were goaded on by anxious traders; and dogs everywhere snarled and fought, for only the aggressive survived. It was here that James first saw the tribespeople from the mountains.

You could hardly miss them. They wore turbans, ornamental sashes and white leggings. The women wore colourful costumes ornamented with shells and beads. They were the 'monkey people', the Chinese said with contempt. They lived perched on the mountains. If local history was correct, however, they were the original inhabitants of much of mainland China, driven south and west by the invaders. Historians estimate there may have been thirty million of them, divided into 150 tribes, each having its own language or' dialect. They had retreated into the mountain fastnesses of Yunnan and neighbouring provinces. (Later, after the Communist take-over in 1949, many migrated to Burma and Thailand.)

James's initial interest in these people sprang from reports of a great turning to God among the tribespeople of East Yunnan, the Miao and Lisu among others. The plan was for James to help in this eastern area as soon as his language studies were completed.

He saw the group of Lisu tribesmen wandering through the market-place and was immediately interested. Drawing alongside, he tried out his Chinese on them. They did not understand a word. However, he guided them towards the little room in the street he called the preaching-hall, and they came gladly. On arrival, they prostrated themselves, knocking their foreheads on the floor repeatedly, overcome with respect for the friendly white-faced stranger. They tried to explain with much gesticulation that they lived six days' journey away in the mountains where there were many of their people.

As he made his way back to the little inn afterwards, climbing the narrow stairs to his room, James's imagination was racing. Might there not be a great turning to God among the Western Lisu, too? He felt like a businessman who has seen a new area of advance. He was surprised, himself, at the immediate affection he felt for these people.

'I was very much led out in prayer for these people, right from the beginning. Something seemed to draw me to them', he said later. But he said nothing about it. In any case, lonely pioneering in the west was a good deal less attractive than joining a team of reapers in the east, if it ever came to that. Besides, as so often with the call of God, it was not an apparently logical step to take. There were teeming millions in the Chinese cities, without lifting one's eyes to the mountains and beyond.

First Solo Journey
One morning soon after this James was up before daybreak dressing by the light of the oil lamp. He wore the clothes of a Chinese coolie for this occasion,

and comfortable sandals for walking, for he was setting off on a four-day trek over the mountains to a Chinese city called Paoshan. He was going on foot because no mule could negotiate the steep inclines nor ford the torrents of the Salween river. He travelled light, carrying only a change of clothes, a blanket and a few small books and tracts.

'I met James Fraser once', remarked an American missionary. 'I had my mule laden with half my things and my coolie's laden with the other half. As we slowly proceeded round the mountain with camp bed, pots and pans and what not, in the middle of nowhere I met James ambling along with a small bag on his back, free as air and happy as a sand boy. I took him for a Chinese coolie at first.'

James sent ecstatic letters home describing the journey from Tengyueh to Paoshan. None of his Alpine climbs could compare with this for stupendous scenery. Sleeping by the stony mountain path and trekking for hours in steadily falling rain, he at last reached the 8,000 foot mountain pass above the Paoshan plain, and after a long descent reached the gates of the city.

Because he was alone in his adventures — apart from a friendly coolie — it was in letters home that he was able to share experiences and talk to friends and family. He describes an exhausting tramp around the city looking for an inn for the night. When at last a landlord granted him a room, James found it was a barn, but he swept it out with a straw brush and thought it quite adequate for his needs. He spread out his dampened clothes to dry over the rafters and set out, dressed in a Chinese gown, to make friends with the people in the streets.

Paoshan

James's first full day in Paoshan was a Sunday, and he
went out of the city to find somewhere for a solitary
time of worship. It was early, and by the time the
dawn mist had cleared he was retracing his steps
toward town again.

Coming to a couple of men minding cattle, I sat
down with them, near a small stream. To my question,
'Have you heard about the Jesus Doctrine?' they
answered, 'No, tell us about it.' So I told them the
Gospel story as clearly as I could. They listened well
and asked questions. A few passers-by stopped and sat
down, so I had to begin over again. More and then
more joined us, until I had told the same thing four or
five times over and about a dozen people were listening.
When the sun came out we all adjourned under a
tree . . . and I went on. Whether they understood all I
was telling them I cannot say, but they listened well
and seemed as interested and friendly as could be. In
getting up once I ripped my gown, and one of them
ran home for a needle and cotton and mended it for
me. I was preaching to them for about an hour and a
half, and then two of them came on with me to lead
me to other places where I could find people to talk
with . . .

Entering the city again in the afternoon, a man in a
teashop saw me distributing tracts and called me to
come in. He gave me a cup of tea and asked to see my
tracts. A crowd soon gathered and I preached to them
as I had been doing all morning. The man who had
called me in seemed fairly well educated. He read the
tracts and listened to all I was saying, evidently
understanding a good deal.

The man who bought him the cup of tea was a
tanner by trade, and he sat for a long time in the
darkened teashop asking questions. His name was

Chao Ho, and he was to be the first in Paoshan to take a stand for Jesus Christ.

Another who showed immediate interest was Wang, the silversmith. Mr Wang was intrigued by the teaching brought by the stranger and he took some trouble to find his inn and invite him to his home to explain it. Mr Wang's table provided food at its best, and over the steaming bowls of rice and vegetables James explained the way of salvation many times.

Mr Wang fixed up a stall in front of his shop and, perched on a stool, James called out his message to the passing crowds. Their interest, their questions and their willingness to accept leaflets made a deep impression on him. Crowds gathered hour after hour to hear this new message. In the political turmoils of the time they had many impassioned revolutionary speakers come and go but they had never heard a message even remotely like this one before.

By the time darkness fell, James was exhausted beyond measure.

After several days of non-stop preaching, he spent a day alone on the hills to get away from the crowds. He sat down in the shadow of a pagoda to shield himself from the searing midday sun.

> It was a lovely day and I had a clear view of the plain in both directions, as well as of the city. Of course, no missionary has ever lived there; and the whole plain, with a population of perhaps 100,000, is without the light of the Gospel . . . I believe God would be glorified by even one witness to His name amid the perishing thousands of Paoshan.
>
> It does seem a terrible thing that so few are offering for the mission field . . . I can't help feeling that there is something wrong somewhere. Surely God must be wanting his people to go forward. Does not the

Master's last command still hold good? . . . As one
thinks of even our corner of the world here in
Yunnan, there seems a strange discrepancy between its
huge districts, large towns, unreached tribespeople,
waiting for the workers who do not come, and the big
missionary meetings at home, the collecting and
subscribing, the missionary literature published, etc.,
etc. And the need is the same, if not greater, in other
parts of the world. Hundreds of millions of people
who have never yet had the Gospel definitely brought
before them — a mere handful of missionaries sent out
from the home countries to evangelize them.

James's use of literature in the Paoshan area proved
fruitful. The Chinese are a thoughtful race and literature is not easily come by. Sometimes he sold the
colourful booklets for a copper or two, and occasionally he gave them out free. Mostly they were copies
of Mark's Gospel, but there were also tracts including
translations of Spurgeon's sermons.

Boy Thief

James had to watch out in the crowded market of
Mangshih, a town south of Paoshan, lest his Bible and
money were stolen as the crowd jostled around him.
Suddenly, someone upset his little trestle table and his
pile of booklets went flying. Some were soaked in
puddles, some trodden down by passing mules and
some whipped up the sleeves of gowns at the speed of
light. There was the flash of a red cover as a six-year-old
child deftly slipped a Mark's Gospel down his shirt and
disappeared in the crowd. It was hardly stealing, the
child thought, since many were given out free — not
that he was over-troubled by moral scruples.

The six year old had actually come to the market on
business. His father was a very successful pastry-cook

and often sent his rich Chinese cakes to the Mangshih market. His name was Moh and he was intelligent and literate. His son knew he would be interested in the booklet. Carefully the lad carried it back over the mountain trail to Hsiangta. More powerful than a two-edged sword, the gospel of Mark began a quiet revolution in that remote mountain home.

Journey into Lisuland

James's interest in the tribal people had not lessened at all, but both he and Embery felt they should wait for an invitation.

> The matter is in the Lord's hands (he wrote). If He wants me to go He will send me. It would be very unwise to attempt to rush things or force a door which He has closed. But we shall see. God has done great things for us at the other side of the province, and we cannot but hope that He will work effectively for the tribespeople here as well.

Several invitations proved abortive; promised guides failed to turn up. Meanwhile, the cook James and Embery employed was beginning to sense their disappointment. The cook was coming into a real understanding of the faith, and often accompanied James on his street-preaching excursions.

> It is dark, he wrote, describing these days, and just as at home, people are at a loose end and wander about with nothing much to do. I get an old stool and stand on it while the cook holds the lantern . . .

One day the cook came back from the market in great excitement. With him came a Lisu guide ready there and then to take James to his Lisu village called Pleasant Valley.

Thus it was that, about a year after his first coming to Tengyueh, James set out on a May morning with his Lisu guide. The journey was on foot westwards, past the rushing Tengyueh waterfall and the slopes where the Temple of the Winds stood, up a trail rising high into the mountains where Lisu territory began.

Pleasant Valley hamlet consisted of about twelve bamboo shanties clinging to the mountainside. There was some excitement in the village, James noticed, as he and his guide climbed the surrounding fence. He soon discovered they were on the eve of a 'betrothal' celebration and all was bustle and jollity. Delighted at their unexpected visitor, the Lisu spread James's bedding on the earth floor by the central log fire and gave him his bowl of rice and eggs.

In the smoky firelight he saw for the first time the happy, hospitable tribespeople he had so much on his heart. Long into the night the talking and laughter went on, the circle round the fire only occasionally broken by the flash of a pinewood chip as a neighbour lit a lamp to return home.

Speaking Paper

The next day James had plenty to observe. The festivity was to be in the evening and all day was spent in preparation. He added to the general merriment by being unable to speak a work of Lisu. They were wide eyed when he started jotting down sounds on paper.

'He's taking away our language', complained one, 'and we shall have nothing to speak.'

By the end of the day James had secured four hundred phrases by means of the English alphabet. This conjuring trick with their language provided endless entertainment to the villagers; they were doubled up with laughter over the speaking paper.

The Chinese had always said that tribal gibberish could not be written down anyway.

By the time the feast was spread I was mighty hungry. Evening had fallen and I had had nothing to eat all day but rice and cabbage for breakfast. So they gave me some food before they actually started themselves — rice and *shanchi* meat, a sort of mountain goat. This was all they had for themselves, except home-made wine, of which they drank copiously . . . There were about fifty at the feast and they sat on boards on the ground in a sort of oblong, the rice and meat being on boards in the centre . . .

The meal was not a sober, ceremonious sort of business, but more like a family party with plenty of jollity. I don't know who the betrothed people were, but they did not figure specially. After the feeding part (I am afraid the drinking went on all night), there was a bit of a break, and I could not make out any order in the proceedings. It was like the game of croquet in *Alice in Wonderland!* I went inside and sat with about a dozen others round the big log fire. One man was recounting an old Lisu legend in a sing-song voice, and the rest would break in with a sort of chorus. I could not understand any of it.

Before long I was told they were ready for the dance, which would be kept up till daylight. What sort of dancing it was to be, I had no idea. My host told me that I could go back to his house whenever I liked, but evidently thought I would wish to stay and see it through.

I was in a corner almost unnoticed. Drinking was going on all the time, while men and women were gobbling, shouting, laughing, some standing up, some sitting down, some going here and there, some outside, some inside, not a few in gaudy-coloured clothing — the setting being a dirty old room in a Lisu house, everything smoked and black, huge grimy

grain-bins here and there, a dog or two running over
the earthen floor and all long after dark in an
aboriginal village in south-west China.

The results of the copious drinking were pre-
dictable. James found no one in any frame of mind to
listen to what he had come to say. But to his surprise, a
man picked his way over the prostrate revellers next
morning with an invitation to his village at Trinket
Mountain, six miles beyond. People there wanted to
learn to read Chinese, he said.

Seven Thousand Feet Up

Pleased at the new opening, James set out for the little
hamlet 7,000 feet up in the mountains. Here he settled
for a week, living on what his host provided — rice
and vegetables twice a day — and sleeping on the earth
floor by the log fire as they did. They were interested
in his message, delivered in simple Chinese. Like
many mountain people, they were innately musical
and loved learning the few Chinese hymns he taught
them.

The Koh family he stayed with were animists, like
most of the tribal people. At the back of their house
was a demon shelf. A bowl of rice, an incense-burner
and a bunch of leaves in which the spirits were
supposed to dwell stood on the shelf. Over it all hung
red paper with the words Heaven and Earth. This
shelf was a powerful reminder that behind the
apparent friendliness of the Lisu and their welcome
to James and his message stood the garrisons of
an alien host. As yet James had little first-hand
knowledge of all that the demon-shelf stood for.

He could not understand the conversation between
the father and his four sons one evening, as it was in

Lisu, but they soon made it clear to him that the demon shelf was to come down. They wanted to please the true God they had been learning about, and His Son Jesus Christ. So, without a word from James, the shelf and its contents were put on the fire in the middle of the room.

He knew they understood very little. 'It was all very happy and nebulous', he wrote home. At least a little light had pierced the gloom of their understanding, though he had to leave them with hardly even a basic grasp of the truth. He little envisaged the sinister turn of events to follow.

Left in Charge

James longed to get back to Tengyueh and share his experiences with Mr and Mrs Embery. He needed someone to share it all with. How deeply he valued their friendship and loving advice! It was a real grief to him now to hear that these senior colleagues of his were to be sent to Tali, and his letters showed how painful he found the experience.

He escorted Mr and Mrs Embery, carrying their baby, for seven miles out of the city and walked back to the empty mission home alone.

> Had it been possible, he wrote, for someone else to go to Tali, the Emberys would not have been asked to do so, but the shortage of workers is so great that no other arrangements could be made . . . As far as matters here are concerned, it means that I am single-handed and must remain so indefinitely. I expect Mr McCarthy will be coming along to stay with me for a time, perhaps next month. I have, however, the responsibility of looking after our comparatively large premises, as well as the much weightier res-

ponsibility of preaching the Gospel alone now. So it
is no small load which has fallen on my shoulders.

James was now in charge of the Tengyueh station.
More than ever before he was, in his loneliness, to
prove the richness of fellowship with God.

Great Testing in Small Things

His present situation was in every sense 'against the
grain'. He did not enjoy housekeeping and looking
after premises. He found the houseboy irritable and
touchy: quarrels constantly flared up between this lad
and the cook. Endless small items of business cluttered
up the time he wanted for language study, and he was
having to learn to be 'perpetually inconvenienced' for
the sake of the gospel. Defeat at this stage of his life
might have led to spiritual stagnation in all the years
ahead. Added to this he longed for a colleague to work
with and share with. He wrote after some weeks alone:

I feel, somehow, that my best opportunity for
Chinese study is gone for ever. Interruptions, visits
and attention to details absorb a good deal of my time.
Not that I deplore this; on the contrary, I am very glad
to be launched into full work as a missionary. It is
what we come to China for. But I am finding out that
it is a mistake to plan to get through a certain amount
of work in a certain time. It ends in disappointment,
besides not being the right way to go about it, in my
judgment. It makes one impatient of interruption and
delay. Just as you are nearly finishing — somebody
comes along to sit with you and have a chat! You
might hardly think it possible to be impatient and put
out when there is such an opportunity for presenting
the Gospel — but it is. It may be just on mealtime or
you are writing a letter to catch the mail, or you were
just going out for needed exercise before tea. But the
visitor has to be welcomed, and I think it is well to

cultivate an attitude of mind which will enable one to welcome him from the heart and at any time. 'No admittance except on business' scarcely shows a true missionary spirit.

And not only so — I have been feeling lately that this personal work is quite as important as preaching. To have a man come to see you at your own house and be able to talk with him plainly and directly about his soul's welfare, what could be better? . . . I feel that there is more force in an appeal under these conditions . . . Of course preaching to crowds must be done, but it is not the only way, in Scripture or out of it, of bringing men to Christ. It may seem a strange thing for a missionary to say, but I feel that if God has given me any spiritual gift it is not that of preaching. I know my own clumsiness and so on very well — but the Lord has always helped me in this one-by-one work and He is giving it to me here.

It is interesting that James did not feel his gift was in preaching, either at home or abroad. In Yunnan, however, preaching tended to be somewhat unstructured. He said he had followed the habits of the irregular preacher at home who was accused of wandering off the subject. 'He replied', James recalled, 'that whether he stuck to his *subject* or not, he thanked God he stuck to his *object*, which was to bring men to Christ. I hope I shall never lose sight of *that*.'

Discouragements and setbacks sometimes laid his spirits low. Enquirers who had shown such interest fell away. The crowds were beginning to get used to his message and passed by indifferently. Some shouted opposition and warned others to steer clear of foreign intruders.

Yet James found God had chosen to make Himself known to unexpected people, quite often older

women. Such was Mrs Li. Only one of her eleven
children had survived childhood, and this one son was
an opium addict like her husband. Out of her hardship Mrs Li had come into a living relationship with
Jesus Christ.

> Listen to what she says: 'I used to be anxious and
> worried about all these things, besides being angry
> and resentful at the way I am treated, but it is not so
> now. If I begin to feel that way I just turn to God, and
> He brings back peace to my heart'.
>
> When I exhort her to pray, she replies, 'Yes, I do
> pray. I am continually thinking about and praying to
> God as I do my work.'
>
> Just a poor, ignorant woman earning her living by
> washing clothes, despised and jeered at by many and
> cruelly ill-treated by her husband, yet daily trusting all
> to her Saviour and praising her God! She nearly cries
> sometimes when she tells me her troubles, but as a rule
> she is bright and cheerful.

Rumblings of Revolution

James was becoming a well-known figure in
Tengyueh, and was even more so when he took an
active part in subduing a fire which threatened to
engulf a major part of the city. The Chinese were
intrigued that the foreigner should show concern for
their people and property when he was not affected
himself. Callers of all kinds came to see him, quite a
few wanting to know his opinion on the impending
overthrow of the Manchu Dynasty. Great were the
hopes pinned on the revolutionary council of Sun Yat
Sen. There were also callers who wanted to talk
philosophy, asking his views on Socrates and
Aristotle. Interested in all these subjects and alive to
every opportunity, James forged several useful friend-

ships in these days before the Revolution of 1911.

News from his Lisu friends was infrequent and discouraging. One of old Koh's sons came in for eye medicine and reported crop failure and poverty in the village. He also said the spirits were active and cruel to the people. But James could not go up there; his duties lay at Tengyueh.

It was increasingly borne home to him that he could probably keep the Tengyueh station going for years quite faithfully and still see very little done for the Lord there. There might even be a slow growth in the work and a faithful witness established. But he somehow felt there was a vast reservoir of power he had as yet hardly begun to tap. He wrote home to his former Class Leader:

> It seems a big responsibility to be the only preacher of the Gospel within a radius of about a hundred and fifty miles . . . I feel my weakness very much, yet the Lord seems to delight in making His power perfect in weakness. May I ask you then to remember me specially in prayer, asking God to use me to the salvation of many precious souls?
>
> I am feeling more and more that it is, after all, just the prayers of God's people that call down blessing upon the work, whether they are directly engaged in it or not. Paul may plant and Apollos water, but it is God who gives the increase; and this increase can be brought down from heaven by believing prayer, whether offered in China or in England. We are, as it were, God's agents — used by Him to do His work, not ours. We do our part, and then can only look to Him, with others, for His blessing. If this is so, then Christians at home can do as much for foreign missions as those actually on the field. I believe it will only be known on the Last Day how much has been

accomplished in missionary work by the prayers of earnest believers at home. And this, surely, is the heart of the problem. Such work does not consist in curio exhibitions, showing slides, interesting reports and so on. Good as they may be, these are only the fringe, not the root of the matter. Solid, lasting missionary work is done on our knees. What I covet more than anything else is earnest believing prayer, and I write to ask you to continue to put up much prayer for me and the work here in Tengyueh.

I should like you continually to pray, not only for the salvation of outsiders but for blessing on those who have definitely accepted Christ . . . I want to be downright in earnest myself, and to be filled with the Spirit.

3 THE BITTER HEIGHTS

Revolution in China

'To Mr Fu, Pastor of the Mission Church in Tengyueh. October 27, 1911.

We respectfully inform you that we have chosen this day as propitious for the overthrow of the present dynasty and the setting up of an independent China.

We are at the same time apprising all your fellow nationals in Tengyueh of the fact, and beseech you not to be alarmed. We will without fail protect you and your property. There is no need for you to send telegrams to any place, either in China or abroad. Please rest assured that you will be quite safe where you are. You will not be molested by anybody.

(Signed by) The Upholders of China as an Independent Country.'

This letter to James, called Fu by the Chinese, heralded the beginning of the successful Republican Revolution of 1911. He was somewhat taken aback by its suddenness, and crossed the town to the Consul's Office. The Consul, the Customs Official and James were the only Europeans in the area at the time. The Consul was well aware of the spirit of rebellion abroad and predicted plenty of bloodshed. It was only eleven years since the Boxer uprising against foreigners which had resulted in the death of many missionaries. White faces might not be welcome on the streets even of an internal revolution. On the Consul's advice James made plans to wait in British Burma until the Revolution was over.

Tengyueh, as it happened, became a battleground between government forces and the rebels. Eventually the government troops defected to the rebel side, but many people died and much property was destroyed in the process.

The cook James employed at Tengyueh agreed to oversee the premises, and James made provision for the language teacher and the house-boy. Then he set out on foot for a rugged eight-day trek over the mountains into Burma. He planned to stay with the Selkirks, a CIM couple working in Bhamo. During his long days of walking he thought with anticipation of the tribal work he might see on the Burma side of the mountains.

Penniless in Burma

Alas, on arrival, after a weary journey, he found the house empty: the Selkirks were away.

He was now in a predicament. He hardly had any money with him and virtually no possessions. His remittance from the Mission was already overdue, but even if it reached Tengyueh during the upheaval, was it likely to reach him in Bhamo, eight days' perilous mountain journey away?

On principle, James did not borrow money nor go into debt. Nor did he feel he should advertize his needs. But he had never been in this position before.

The Selkirks had left a note with their caretaker inviting any visiting missionary to use the stores in their larder. By living with the utmost economy James had food for the first week or two, but by the end of the month the supply was running dry, and besides, he had to pay his coolie.

Day after day he called at the Post Office. No letters. What did he expect during such a time of turmoil? asked the clerk.

The promises of God to supply our needs ran constantly through his mind. He was on his knees day after day asking God to send his remittance safely through so that he could pay his coolie. He underlined Psalm 37. 3-5 in his Bible as the day approached when the coolie would expect payment.

Nothing had arrived by the day in question. James went again to the Post Office.

The clerk was all smiles. Yes, there was a registered letter from Shanghai, forwarded from Tengyueh. It contained the draft for his money! God had watched over the small packet on its 1,600 mile journey, through revolutionary turmoil and natural hazard to reach a poor servant of His in his hour of need. A good and just Employer! What's more, he was able to get one of the drafts cashed that very day.

> I have since heard (he wrote to his mother) that the money was paid in full in Tengyueh to the firm here which advanced it to me. I have told you all this because it is the most direct interposition of God in providence which I have yet experienced, and has done not a little to strengthen my faith. No one here knew my situation. You can understand how very careful I am as to speaking of such matters . . . The Lord, I believe, permitted the trial just to show me how He could deliver me out of it.

Lone Traveller

James's days in Bhamo tended to be lonely, although he spent plenty of time in the teashops talking the gospel to Chinese residents.

> I just sat down on a bench with the others, paid a halfpenny for a cup of tea and started cracking pine-

seeds like the rest . . . Soon the guests were chatting to
me, asking lots of questions.

Eventually he set out southwards for Namkham: a
hot jungle journey of several days. The tropical forests
were full of monkeys, green parrots and exquisite
pheasants; but the trees soon gave way to open
mountain scenery, rolling range after range towards
the borders of Yunnan.

Here he met tribal Christians of the Shan and the
Kachin. The Shan states stretch away to the south, the
famous opium-growing area which became a vital
source of supply in worldwide narcotic trading. The
Kachin country is the high, barren mountain area of
the China-Burma border. The warmth of these
Christian tribespeople met an eager response from the
lonely traveller. He could only speak through an
interpreter, but he enjoyed fellowship even when he
could not understand a word of their services or
conversation.

Mrs Sam Bwa, a Shan schoolmaster's wife showed
James a caring affection he had not had since leaving
England. She had noticed his meagre outfit, and her
motherly heart was touched. Unobtrusively she fitted
into his pack a little embroidered pillow, a plate,
spoon and fork, some tea, sugar and biscuits. 'When I
tried to tell Mrs Sam Bwa how grateful I felt for all her
kindness she made no reply, but turned her head away
to hide her tears.'

James looked back on his visit here as one of the
happiest of his early years in the work.

> You can hardly understand until you come into
> touch with them what simple, warm-hearted people
> these Shan and other Christians are. Sam Bwa told me
> that I could be of help to them even if I could say

nothing . . . the mere fact of your coming to see them, showing yourself genuinely pleased to sit with them in their houses, attend their services, share their food and generally make yourself one with them is enough to endear you to them. If I sing or pray in Chinese, they cannot understand a word — but that makes no difference! They like me to do it. They do not judge you by the learning or eloquence of your 'discourse', but by what they see of you personally. If they see that you love them and like to be with them, they love you in return.

He was able to visit some of the Kachin Christians on his way back to Bhamo, and spoke through an interpreter at their tiny chapel.

Afterwards we all sat round the log-fire. Talk about your 'Grand Hotel'! I had rather sleep in a simple homely place like that, among such people, than in the grandest of hotels at home. But our Kachin friends did not stay on indefinitely. They said I had walked a long way and must be wanting rest, which was thoughtful. So they went away and left us in silence, with the fire dying down. I turned in, and soon fell into a sound sleep beside the dull red logs.

Return to China

It was not long before James was able to return to Tengyueh. He found an uneasy calm in the city, and his property and helpers unharmed. China was now a Republic and the people hoped for reforms which were long overdue.

James settled down to the last part of his prescribed language study and was glad to finish it a few months after his return. Not that he did not enjoy the study. 'If I were to be mainly engaged in work among Chinese-speaking peoples (rather than the tribes) I would never give up the study of this language as long as I live', he

wrote. He was a diligent student, and he was later
regarded as one of the CIM experts in the language.

To his great delight, James was now joined by an
American, Carl Gowman, fresh from the Ford head
office in Detroit and trained at the Moody Bible
Institute. The same age as James, Carl was a 'live wire'
and ready for anything. He was impressed with the
snowy heights around them and keen to see something
of the tribes.

> He was a bright, delightful companion, just the
> one I was needing (James wrote of this new
> colleague). He caught on to my interest in the Lisu,
> and joined me in prayer for fresh openings among
> them. I was more burdened about these people than
> anything else in the world, though the duties of the
> station, the claims of Chinese study and the upheaval
> of the Revolution had kept me from further contact
> with them.

James and Carl were up before 6 a.m. for an early
morning swim in the river, and then they had household prayers. It was a stimulus to James to have Carl
to pray with in detail about the work, and to have a
partner to discuss plans with. He also enjoyed
initiating Carl into Chinese customs and their way of
life.

But there were many aspects of life, hidden from
James's Victorian mother and his friends at home,
that Carl found himself faced with. He soon got used
to seeing most women hobbling on their tiny bound
feet, but one could not get used to the screams of little
girls whose feet were broken for this purpose (the idea
being that they would never marry if their feet were
large). He had to steel himself to witness other
cruelties from time to time.

Death of a Slave

As Carl and James walked down the centre street one day they heard shouting and angry voices. A little slave girl was being beaten for some misdemeanour. The two young missionaries stopped to investigate and noticed she was seriously ill. The crowd would not let James intervene: it was none of his business.

A few hours later James returned and asked after the child.

'She's dead,' said a man sweeping the courtyard. He jerked his chin, 'over there, in the mortuary.'

James crossed to the mortuary and the caretaker allowed him to see the wooden box where her body lay. James levered the lid off and felt the child's pulse: it was faintly beating. He took the box out into the fresh air and the child opened her eyes.

The caretaker was anxious and angry now. 'Your house will be burnt down if they find a foreigner has touched anything here', he remonstrated.

James carried the child home in his arms. They laid her on a bed and he and Carl gave her a little drink. For the next few days they cared for the flickering life with great tenderness. And with bachelor enthusiasm, they planned how they would adopt her, bring her up and pay for her schooling.

But it was not to be. The child died a week later, only one of the hundreds of little unwanted girls in the city.

Silver Pheasant Bribe

One morning soon after this James's door stood open to the morning sun, and as he looked out he was surprised to see a silent figure on the steps, silhouetted against the mountains. It was a Lisu tribesman. As James went out to greet him he saw a flash of colour.

The man had a live silver pheasant in his hand, which
he had caught in the mountains. He wanted James to
accept the brilliant bird as a gift, but he also wanted to
borrow ten dollars for a family wedding, and invited
him to come as a guest.

James was in something of a quandary. He never
lent money. But he invited the Lisu in, and while he
talked to Carl, James went to his room to pray about
the situation. It was not long before he came down
assured and handed over the ten dollars.

The Tsai family made splendid preparations to
receive James, Carl and the cook at the wedding. No
planning permission was needed to extend their
bamboo house on the mountainside: a lean-to exten-
sion provided an adequate guest room. It was thatched
with grass, a hole dug in its centre for a fire and a pile
of pine chips provided for lights.

Six Family Hollow was only a tiny hamlet of three
families, and Carl and James had a few days there
before the wedding festivities began. They found old
mother Tsai very much head of affairs. Her first
husband had died, leaving land and children, so she
had married again and through industry and business
acumen had brought prosperity to her family. She was
intelligently interested in James's message straight
away, and in spite of all the business of the wedding
preparations would sit and listen intently, showing
real hunger after God.

Mountain Wedding

The wedding itself was a colourful affair, character-
ized by much drinking of the intoxicating rice wine.
The bridegroom, James wrote, looked fine, 'something like a Highlander in full dress.' The great
moment was when the bride entered the house.

Then her mother-in-law and another old dame went down and escorted her, one on each side, up the steps and into the house. There was a bridesmaid with her too. Just as they were going in at the door, four shots were fired by muskets of a William the Conqueror type, this being *the* moment of the whole occasion.

There was much bowing and much drinking to the health of the couple followed by ring-dancing and a strange kind of clog-dancing.

Three girls, one boy and a man stood in a line, the girls with their arms round each other. Further away was another boy, the bride's mother with a kind of guitar, and beyond him, another man. They all faced the same way and, without turning, just kept step to the music. I should like you to have seen it! The dress of the girls beggars description. Indeed, all the women wear gorgeous dresses on occasion . . . Some of them look very handsome. They go in for very loud chequerwork, with large squares of all sorts of colours. They have big head-dresses too, and a great variety of beads, bangles, necklaces, bracelets and what not!

Carl and James politely declined the intoxicant, but were each given a large lump of cold pork fat to eat.

Gowman, I believe, ate his, but they brought me a plantain leaf in which I wrapped mine.

The revelry lasted two days and two nights, the hundred or so guests becoming increasingly drunk and proceedings increasingly confused. In a sort of stupor they listened on and off as Carl and James played their tiny portable organ and sang, trying to explain to them the message of the Cross. But it was not until the wedding was over and the guests had gone that they were able to get down to serious work.

The Tsai Family
Snow was falling on the upper ranges as the Tsai

family gathered round their indoor fire to listen to
James and Carl. Dogs, chickens and pigs, as well as
toddlers and children wandered in and out while the
organ played and discussions went on. Mother Tsai in
particular wanted to grasp the truth and believe. She
was full of questions and thinking deeply, and James
found his good friend the cook indispensable in
explaining it all to her.

They stayed there for a week, in the meantime
visiting the Kohs again at Trinket Mountain. Only
the old father was there, in pain with eye trouble, but
he was glad to see James and begged him to stay. But
the sons were away, and James promised to come later.
Carl was already finding tribal travels telling on him,
and James knew they must soon get him back to
Tengyueh for a rest. The rough life-style and inade-
quate food would take some getting used to.

Their last night was spent with the Tsai family at
Six Family Hollow. They really believed, they said,
that Jesus was the Son of God and had made atone-
ment for them. They really wanted to join His family,
the people of God. They did not know how to pray in
Lisu, they said, but would God mind if they prayed in
broken Chinese? They could sing the hymns they had
learnt, couldn't they? They would come down to
Tengyueh to visit James and learn more.

Encouraged, James and Carl returned over the
mountains to Tengyueh. How palatial the mission-
house seemed now! How soft the beds, how royal the
food, and how clean it all looked!

A Church with Four
In Tengyueh itself the little church was getting going,
and for the first time they were to have four people
baptized. Mrs Li was to be baptized on Mrs Embery's

reutrn, but James took the three men — the cook, a
water carrier and a teacher — down to a quiet stretch
of river near the Tengyueh falls by a bridge where
onlookers could see it all.

> After the baptism I stood where I was in the middle
> of the river and preached to the onlookers on the
> bridge . . . It struck me afresh what a beautiful and
> simple ceremony it is — God's open air and God's
> flowing water seemed far more fitting and natural
> than any baptistry indoors.

The little group then went back and shared the
bread and wine, symbols of the body and blood of the
Lord Jesus. It was a memorable joy. There was a little
flock now to be cared for, the first group of believers in
that corner of south-west China.

Plenty of things were now crowding in on James's
time. Although he had disciplined himself never to let
a day go by without going out to preach in the streets
or the markets, he found everything to deter him from
doing so. It was a battle to do the thing he had come to
China to do.

> When utterly disinclined to go and stand up on a
> stool in the street and preach to an indifferent crowd, I
> have felt an inward urging which I could not resist. It
> is like so much pent-up Gospel inside you, which
> must have outlet. Last week, on Friday, I was
> prevented from going out as usual to preach, and tried
> to satisfy myself with the resolve to do so next day
> instead. But on Saturday the very same thing
> happened, and by the time for the evening prayer
> meeting I had let another day go by without this
> witness. But I felt just as ill at ease as could possibly
> be. All my peace of mind was gone . . . and I was
> impatient for the meeting to be over.
> When it ended, I could stand the conflict no longer,
> but had to go out on the main street, late though it

was, get up on a form and give my message to the
people. This done, I was as happy as could be! . . . It is
a fine thing to have God call you to work with Him,
isn't it? But finer still, I think, to have Him make you
do it.

But in spite of all the calls on his time, he found the
Lisu increasingly on his heart. He wished day after
day that he could spare time to visit them again.
However, on market days they came down from the
mountains and made a habit of calling on him. He
wrote of one such occasion when members of the Tsai
family called:

> I enjoyed the evening they stayed here immensely.
> Their simple ingenuousness attracts me tremen-
> dously. They take you into their confidence as if you
> were an old friend of the family. The boy who married
> while we were up there learnt a new hymn this time,
> one of Pastor Hsi's, which they like very much. This
> brings their repertoire to the grand total of three. They
> religiously rattle through these hymns every evening
> (!) by way of evening prayers, after which all the
> family stand up to pray. They tell me they can pray in
> Lisu now. On Sunday evenings (dear simple souls!)
> they try to have an extra special kind of service. There
> is nothing very much extra that they can manage, but
> anyway they sing a little more than usual, and try to
> make out what the hymns are all about. Crude, isn't
> it? But I wonder if the Lord is not just as pleased with
> their simple, groping attempts at worshipping Him
> as with our elaborate services at home? 'Out of the
> mouths of babes and sucklings Thou hast perfected
> praise.'
>
> 'Old Six', as the bridegroom is called, stopped in
> the middle of learning this hymn with me.
> 'I say, Teacher,' he interposed, 'it has been fine
> since we became Christians! The evil spirits don't get
> after us now, like they used to. People say that most of
> the Lisu up at the Valley of Ease are waiting to see if

anything happens to our Tsai family. If not, many of
them want to be Christians too.'

The Face of the Enemy

James was now entering into a whole theatre of
warfare for which he was unprepared. The prince of
this world does not easily cede his territory to the
people of God. The mountains had been the strong-
hold of Satan for countless centuries: they were not to
be lightly invaded. Persuasion to pay half-hearted lip-
service to God for a while would be a relatively
harmless exercise; it could co-exist with a demon shelf
anyway. But if the Spirit of the Living God were to
regenerate the hearts of these people and set up His
Kingdom there, it would be another matter; it would
demonstrate the victory won on the Cross. The enemy
would make an onslaught against any such possibility.
He would attack the messenger, his message and all
who gave ear to it.

The Tsai family had been singing their hymns one
evening when the old father brought up the question
of the demon-shelf. His family at once decided it was
time to burn it and burn it they did. That night,
however, the old man was seized with a back pain
which soon spread to the whole of his body. Such was
his agony, the whole family was up trying to relieve
it. Eventually they decided to ask God about it. After
the prayer, the old man's pain eased, and gradually it
went away altogether. This was a great bulwark to
their faith. But there was still a shadowy fear of the
demons and their power to wreak vengeance. When
James heard this story he assured them that the Name
of Jesus is above every name. His victory is already
won: just claim it, he said. But he was disturbed by the
incident.

Little River

Soon after this he found himself freed sufficiently to
set out on a Lisu journey. He wanted to see how
things were progressing in the places he had already
visited and he wanted to master the Lisu language.
Everywhere he found the people warm and friendly
towards him, not to say curious. He wrote during this
trip, which he made in the company of Old Five of the
Tsai family:

> I had a good time at Little River. It is only a tiny
> village of six families, the simplest people you ever
> saw. We were there for four days. I had the luxury of a
> room to myself — oh, no, not private! Privacy is a
> thing almost unheard of out here. The 'walls' of these
> houses, made only of bamboo laths, let in more than
> the free, fresh air! . . . People come around you all the
> time, asking endless questions, wanting to see your
> things and spitting their red betel-nut all over the
> floor. You think it is blood when you first see it. But I
> do not mind even this. I think I like almost everything
> about them but their spit! They are just like children
> and you love them as such.

They would feel his clothes, look through his bags,
sit on his sleeping mat and watch him write. They
were puzzled about his being 26 and unmarried. They
longed to see an English woman: the man who had
seen Mrs Embery had plenty of legendary tales to tell.
Perhaps they could get him a Lisu wife — the very best
they could find in the mountains, they assured him.
They sensed, these people of Little River, that his life
was, humanly speaking, a very solitary one.

For this reason, the Lisu acceptance of him was
especially treasured. For many days James and Old
Five stayed on at Little River teaching the villagers the
essentials of the gospel. Old Five was able to help

them pray in Lisu and James taught them simple hymns to sing. The people warmed to the message. They accepted the truth of the teachings of Jesus, they said, and wanted to 'turn Christian'. Could they not build a chapel for Jesus as they had built that demon-shrine standing up there on the hillside?

> It was a poor, wretched little place, with a thatched roof and open on all four sides. There were no idols in it, for the Lisu are not idolaters. In fact, there was nothing in it but a rough shelf on which they put offerings of food when the spirits came and harassed them. Old Five and I enquired whether they would be willing to give this up. After consultation, they said they would give up anything which was inconsistent with their becoming Christians — so we could do what we liked with the shelf. So Old Five and I went up . . . and it did me good to see him wrench it from its place and fling it away, crying, 'What have we Christians to do with fear of demons?' I wrote an inscription in Chinese on a small cross-beam, above the place the shelf had occupied, to make their change more definite.

Every morning and every evening they would all meet together and worship the God of heaven and earth. A leader was appointed to conduct the worship. At first they felt this God must be localized. What would happen to them if they were minding cattle up on the mountains for a few nights and could not be at the worship? James explained that God would love to hear the Lisu herdsmen pray to Him up in the mountains. They were His mountains after all. He made them.

Attack on the Koh Family
With lightened step, James and Old Five left Little River, promising to pray daily for these young believers

and to return soon. They set out for Trinket Mountain
to visit the Koh family again. It was a steep uphill
climb, every exertion rewarded with a breath-taking
view. The toil and sweat of scratching a living from
the poor soil left little time and interest for scenic
beauty in the Lisu mind — or the Chinese coolie's
either, for that matter. But Old Five was beginning to
learn how much mountain beauty meant to James as
they climbed up to the village, stopping now and then
to drink it all in.

Old Koh's wrinkled face looked tired, James
thought, as he saw him squatting in the doorway.
When the old man rose to greet him and led him
inside, the room looked bare and empty. Maybe the
crops have failed, James thought.

Family and friends soon gathered in the house, and
James and Old Five struck up with some singing. But
the singing seemed lethargic, and a discussion had
started in the far end of the room. Gradually James
sensed that tension was mounting. Koh Three seemed
to be objecting. It soon became clear that James could
not carry on, and a general argument was taking place
in rapid Lisu that he could not understand.

The meeting broke up and although he stayed the
night he was not able to fathom the situation. It was
not until the next day, as they made their way down
the mountainside, that Old Five sat down and with a
troubled heart poured out the story.

> He said that when I was up there for the first time,
> the Kohs believed all I told them and decided to pray
> to God and to the Lord Jesus. At that time there were
> four sons living at home. Not long after, the youngest
> son fell ill. In accordance with my teaching, they
> prayed for his recovery — some of them, at any rate,
> seem to have done so. But the sickness only became

worse. Apparently they continued praying, though whether they resorted to any of their old ways, I cannot tell. The boy continued to sink — until in desperation, they felt that something else must be done. So they stopped praying and sent for a "diviner" who told them that the illness was due to 'spirit seizure'. He told them what to offer to appease the spirit — pig, fowl or whatever it was. They offered it, and from that time the boy began to recover.

Nothing happened after that for a while. Then the storm broke.

Koh Three is a timid, mild kind of youth. You would never expect anything unusual or violent from him. But one evening he and his younger brother 'went mad'. He got a big winnowing basket and beat it as if it were a gong, raving all the time and scaring everybody. Then these two scrambled up on to the *chia-t'ang* (a long narrow table occupying the place of honour, below the ancestral tablets), raving like madmen. To his aged father, Koh Three shouted: 'Come along here and worship me *(kotow)* or I am going to die.'

The younger brother began to stuff his mouth with rice — only done when people are at the point of death, to give them something to eat in the next world. Frightened out of his senses, the old man went up and made humble obeisance before his sons. They continued raving. Then Koh Three seized an incense bowl made of earthenware, shouting in demoniacal fury:

'I will show you earth people whether I have power or not!'

Whereupon he flung it violently on the ground and it did not break. After this paroxysm had passed, the younger brother was very ill again. In spite of all they could do, he gradually sank and died.

Later on, another brother, Koh Two, went out into the fields one day and in anger for something or other scolded his wife, upon which she went back and

committed suicide, by taking opium. After this Koh
Two ran away and has never been heard of since. All
this has happened, they believe, because they forsook
the worship of the spirits and turned to God and
Jesus.

'Do you remember,' Old Five questioned, 'what a
big family it used to be? There seems nothing left of
them now.'

And when I realize the point of view they take
about such things, my wonder is not that they have
been in seldom to see us, but that they come at all.

James was not slow to discern the face of Satan.
It was, after all, Mark's gospel that Old Koh had
first read, with no fewer than ten references to the
casting out of devils in the first six chapters. But this
was a new confrontation for James, and he was deeply
exercised over it.

Thinking over the whole matter it almost seems to
me that it is explained by Luke 11.24-26. After a
lifetime of service to the Evil One, these people tried,
in a blundering way, to break free and worship God,
through Jesus Christ. Then came the trial of their
faith. Satan raged. He got his knife into those who
dared to question his authority in his Lisu kingdom.
He was successful. Old habits and superstitions got
the better of feeble faith . . . His rebels gave him back
their allegiance. First, then, for the candy, to show
what a kind master he is — the boy got better; then
with sevenfold fury for the whip.

In spite of the convictions growing upon him
James was still slow to believe that demon-possession
can be as real today as when our Lord was upon
earth. And yet, why not?

You may call it imagination if you like, but from
the Scriptures we know that Satan is 'the god of this
world' now, as much as he ever was. 'The whole world

lieth in the evil one.' The thing which made it so
painful to me was that the Lisu, in their ignorance,
put all the trouble down to their attempt to become
Christians instead of the very opposite, their reversion
to demon-worship. And the finishing touch, to me,
was the way it shook the faith of Old Five to hear
about it all.

Day of Adversity

James's evangelistic excursions into Lisu territory had
seemed so fruitful, and the people so responsive, that
the new development brought the shock of a sudden
insight. Back in Tengyueh he gave himself to prayer.
He was absorbed in Chinese city work for some weeks,
but looked out of his westward windows daily towards
the mountains, hoping for visitors from his Lisu
villages.

Then one morning Old Five arrived, and it was
clear why no Lisu had been to see him.

I cannot tell you all of it (James wrote in sorrow)
but the evil one has been terribly busy. The result is
that the Tsai family, with the exception of Old Five,
have gone back to their old life and superstitions.

While I was away, their eldest grandson was taken
ill with fever. A little quinine would probably have
put him right, but instead of coming to us for
medicine, as I had arranged in case of need, they
listened to their neighbours and called in a wizard. It
was the spirit, he told them, outraged by the pulling
down of that bunch of leaves, who had come to take
his revenge. Thereupon they put up a big bunch of
leaves again and promised to sacrifice a pig to the
spirits. This they will do as soon as they can afford it.
Down came the hymns, the coloured tracts, etc., and
the Christian books were put away. They have stopped
singing and praying.

Of the whole family, Old Five only seems to hold
fast. The others have made a complete renunciation,

at any rate for the present. They do not object to his
still being a Christian if he likes but they are going to
bide their time: perhaps later on if it seems safe, etc.
This, of course, is Satan's argument. I cannot tell you
how I feel about it — you must use your imagination.
But I am going to pray for them as much as ever. Will
you?

The news had an almost physical effect on James.
All his labours had apparently come to nothing. All
his hopes and encouragements had proved abortive.
He wished he had not written to Mr Hoste in
Shanghai in such glowing terms about the beginnings
of a work among the Lisu. There was virtually
nothing there now: the Tsais, it seemed, had gone
back, but for Old Five, and even he was wavering; the
Kohs had renounced their new faith; and now he had
news from Little River.

They tell me (he continued) that the people at
Little River, who were so responsive when I was there,
have gone back too. They say that after I left a lot of
them fell sick, so they all veered over to their demon
worship again. Whether this is wholly true I do not
know. If it is so, may God forgive them, for they know
not, or can hardly know, what they do.

James was deeply cast down. He was still designated
to the work in the east of the province, and his time
was running out. 'I should desperately like to see the
foundation of a real work here before I leave', he wrote
at the time. But the harvest in the east was crying out
for reapers and the crops seemed to have failed in the
west.

James was glad he had Carl to share things with.
Carl was soon to be married, and the prospect
brightened the mission house considerably. And just
at this time when he was so sorely tried over the Lisu

work, God sent him great comfort in the coming of Ba
Thaw.

Ba Thaw was a 23-year-old Karen from Burma,
who spoke fluent English as well as Lisu. He was
well-educated but, more importantly, a deeply-taught
and spiritually-minded man. His presence was like
water in a thirsty land. He spent some days encouraging the Tengyueh band and also talking to some Lisu
visitors who called. And then he accompanied Old
Five back to his village and spent several days with the
Tsai family, among others, teaching them clearly
from the Bible that the devil was a liar from the
beginning. His loving counsel was well received and
James took heart again.

Reconnaissance Climbing

Meanwhile a letter came from Mr Hoste in
the Shanghai HQ suggesting that a survey should be
made of the area that so interested James. Just how
many tribes were there? Where were they? What
problems of language and terrain would have to be
faced?

And so it was that he set out on a six-week
reconnaissance survey of the whole mountainous
region, north, west and south. Old Five was to come
with him, a useful interpreter and companion. James
wore his cotton jacket and trousers, cotton leggings to
protect from leeches and thorns, and sandals on his feet.
Apart from a little literature for distribution and a
couple of blankets for the night, there was little to carry.

It was a journey into virgin territory, over ranges no
European had traversed before. For days James and Old
Five plodded on, trying to chart the distance between
village and village, many of which consisted of a few
bamboo huts clinging to dark ravines eight thousand

feet above the thundering gorges of the Salween river.
As it was still the rainy season, they had to cross streams
and rivers on ropes or floating planks, and often they
found themselves ploughing through mud over a foot
deep. 'But at least', James wrote, 'it is clean mud, very
different from the filthy, slimy, dark green stuff round
cattle pens and pig sties.'

Rats for Dinner
Cold and hunger were constant companions. Sometimes they caught and ate mountain rats or weasels;
sometimes they were able to buy rice and eggs at a
village. Bitter winds blew over the passes, and they
welcomed the smoky fires of the villages at night. James
found he was in his natural element, 'sitting down in a
poor little place among utter strangers, thousands of
miles from home and several days' journey from the
nearest European, warming my wet clothes and
looking out on a silent world of mist, rain and
mountains, feeling just as happy as could be — even
thrilled with pleasure to think of it.'

In every village James told the story of Jesus Christ.
In a place called Tantsah, he had a specially warm
reception. There were over a hundred families there
and he was welcomed to stay and talk with the villagers.

> People were in and out all day (he wrote of this
> hospitality). In the evening we had splendid services.
> The room was jammed to overflowing —men, boys
> and women with their breast ornaments, beads and
> babies, all squeezing in to listen. Attention was often
> rapt and response hearty.
> 'Yes, yes,' they would break in, 'we all want to be
> Christians!' Then, after the meeting there would be a
> veritable Babel — a crowd round the table, trying to
> read our Chinese Gospels, another round the fire, all
> laughing and talking away . . . To add to the confusion

someone would bring out his guitar and get up a
dance! And I would fall asleep at last, dead tired, with
more people round the bed examining my mosquito
curtains.

It was during this survey that the hold demonism
had over these people came home to James. This was
not a childish belief in something non-existent. The
demons were real: their power was demonstrable. The
fear the villagers lived in amounted to total slavery. In
one village of the Tantsah area the demon-priests were
forced to propitiate 'the great spirit' from time to time
by getting volunteers to walk up a ladder of sharpened
sword blades. After being purified, the victims ascended
the ladder naked, and in a trance.

> They all tell me that no man so 'prepared' is ever
> injured, though they frequently suffer from fear before-
> hand. They say, too, that no one 'unprepared' would
> dare attempt it, for the blades would just about cut his
> feet in pieces. When at the top on a kind of platform,
> they look down with glaring eyes and in unearthly
> tones give messages from the spirit. At times they make
> a huge fire also, in which they burn iron chains until
> red hot — then in some kind of paroxysm they pick
> them up and throw them round their shoulders. In this
> case also they say that no harm comes to them. You
> might suppose that onlookers regard the whole thing
> as a kind of entertainment but this is far from the case.
> They all say that they wish they knew how to get rid of
> the burden; but they must do it, whether they want to or
> not. Last year, only one man was found 'pure enough'
> to go through it. I saw this man's father and the little
> home up on the mountain-side where they allow
> themselves to be drawn into the diabolical vortex.

James watched all this in silence. Had he under-
estimated the enemy? But 'for this cause was the Son of
God manifested, that He might destroy the works of the
devil.' (I John 3.8)

There were some touching examples of hunger for
the true God. A poor, bent old woman sought him out
in a tiny shop as he was talking to a group of men. Her
face besought him. She had heard him say in his
preaching that demon and idol worship was full of lies.
'Please, please tell me what is true,' she whispered.
James spent some time with her explaining the way of
salvation in Christ. 'I feel at peace now', she said
quietly. 'Ten-tenths at peace.'

The busy keeper of an inn pleaded with James to
teach her how to pray to the Living God. She seemed to
grasp the meaning of the Cross. Over and over again
she repeated the little prayer he taught her. Next
morning, while it was still dark, she was up looking for
him. 'Say it for me again', she begged. 'I want so much
to pray, and there will be no one to help me when you
have gone.'

Many were the experiences of this survey. Once or
twice James and Old Five passed hamlets where in-
breeding had resulted in mental retardation affecting
the whole group. Most villages had their tribe of savage
dogs to ward off strangers: snarling, emaciated creat-
ures more effective than a city wall. James faced an
onslaught from a pack of these hounds one day and was
badly mauled by the time Old Five had helped beat
them off with sticks. They bound up his bleeding legs
and feet, but it was in real pain that he hobbled into the
village, to the amusement of the villagers. Well, he
thought, his feet were not exactly beautiful now, even
though on the mountains bringing the gospel of peace.

The Kachin Tribes

In coming south again, James was skirting the wild
Kachin country.

> They are the wildest people round here by a long way (he reported). Inveterate robbers, their hand is against every man and every man's hand is against them. Dirty, unkempt, ignorant, everybody despises them. They are savages only and not cannibals.

On one of the hills as they approached the area, three Kachin tribesmen shot arrows at them. In good cowboy fashion they sheltered among the rocks until their assailants had gone.

There were plenty of brigands in the mountains, and on more than one occasion in his missionary career James was to be robbed of all but his underclothes. Old Five was worried occasionally, on this reconnaissance trip, as to how he and James would fight them off. James assured him they would let the brigands take their things without resisting: God would supply all they needed if they were left with nothing.

In actual fact, the wild Kachin warmed to his gentle approach, allowing him to sleep in their little shacks at night, and a friendship was forged during this trip that later bore much spiritual fruit.

The Report Received

On his return, James sent a fourteen-page report to Mr Hoste in Shanghai. In the northern area alone there were 300 towns and villages and a population of 10,000 Lisu, and even greater numbers of Kachin. The Shan area he had not yet begun to chart. James was deeply moved at the extent of the need.

For some days he lay in his bed in Tengyueh in a state of total exhaustion, and malarial fever set in to weaken him even more. His legs had ulcers and were causing him real pain. Mental and spiritual depression was the natural outcome. And his dread was a letter from HQ sending him to the east, though why he

should dread it he did not know. There was a happy
and united team working among responsive tribal
people in the eastern province. His own western area
had no one but himself, and there seemed little response
to his preaching.

The bitter blow was not long in coming. A letter
came from Mr Hoste telling him that the eastern work
had prior claim: he was to go to Sapushan, in the east of
the province.

Able to Accept
In acceptance there is peace.

> I was not staggered by unbelief (he could say,
> recalling that painful experience). I did not know what
> to make of it, for God had given me such a burden for
> the Lisu, and a growing conviction that He was
> leading. So I just went on praying about it — as much
> and as happily as before — though a good deal
> perplexed.

He did not talk to anyone about it. But it was a test
that proved his inner strength. He was willing to go.

Meanwhile, during the grey days of convalescence,
James still prayed incessantly for his Lisu flock. He
looked forward eagerly to market days when they called
to see him, desperately concerned that the young
believers should stand firm in the faith.

> This evening Old Five has come in again . . . He
> brings good news of his family. They all seem to want
> to stand firm now, with the one exception of his elder
> brother. They have thrown away that bunch of leaves
> they put up some months ago and have 'prayers' again
> every morning. And he tells me that the sick people I
> prayed for at Little River — and for whom I have
> prayed ever since, hoping very, very much that they
> might be spared — have both recovered. We have been
> talking over our recent trip together and how the Lisu

gave us ready hearing everywhere . . .

And last but not least, Old Five himself seems to be holding fast and growing in grace, so that he has played the part of an angel in banishing the gloom from my spirit. Like Paul, refreshed by the coming of Timothy with good news of the Thessalonians, I too can cry after a season of despondency, 'Now we *live*, if ye stand fast in the Lord.'

Meanwhile Carl Gowman's bride arrived and the wedding took place with much rejoicing among their Chinese friends. The Gowmans then left for their honeymoon and James stayed alone in the mission house to await the Emberys' return. He had time to spend in prayer.

Decision of a Lifetime

It was not many days after this that a telegram arrived from Mr Hoste in Shanghai. James had to read it several times to take it in.

'If you feel distinctly led to stay on for Lisu work, I would not press your going to Sapushan.'

Although the team in the east of the province were in dire need of more workers, they generously recognised the need in the west and had agreed that James should explore his field further.

It was a winter's night when he climbed the hill to the deserted temple, a favourite prayer-haunt. He needed time to pray with an uncluttered mind. Was he right in feeling he should stay on at Tengyueh? Was it the right time for western Lisu work? The old temple-priest listened as James prayed aloud.

I walked up and down in the moonlight, praying aloud in the silence, until prayer was turned to praise. There was no longer any question. Committing myself to God for whatever might be His Purpose, I decided to stay on in my Tengyueh field.

4 ONE WEAPON ONLY

A Letter Home

James now began to assess the size of his task. He wasn't afraid of arduous climbing nor of primitive living, because he loved mountaineering anyway. But the prospect of working alone to build a living church to stand against such a powerful form of spirit-worship was daunting. He knew the hosts of God stood with him. But he also knew that there was no such thing as a solo worker in God's plan. He had, of course, the Mission support behind him, but clearly no-one could be spared to go with him as yet; everyone was involved in Chinese work and stretched to the limit. But he now wrote home about a new kind of partnership.

> I know you will never fail me in the matter of intercession (he wrote to his mother), but would you think and pray about getting a group of like-minded friends, whether few or many, whether in one place or scattered, to join in the same petitions? If you could form a small prayer circle I would write regularly to the members.

This was the first suggestion of such partners in his work, and it was acted upon immediately back in Letchworth. In ones and twos people in the area of his home agreed to share the burden with him. They undertook the task much as a business partnership: it was a clear and definite commitment to the job. They would pray him through.

What a number of earnest, spiritually-minded Christians there are at home and how correspondingly rich are the prayer forces of the Church! How I long for some of this wealth for myself and the Lisu here. Yes, I have had it in measure already . . . but I should very, very much like a wider circle of intercessors.

Our work among the Lisu is not going to be a bed of roses, spiritually. I know enough about Satan to realize that he will have all his weapons ready for determined opposition. He would be a missionary simpleton who expected plain sailing in any work of God. I will not, by God's grace, let anything deter me from going straight ahead in the path to which He leads, but I shall feel greatly strengthened if I know of a definite company of pray-ers holding me up. I am confident that the Lord is going to do a work, sooner or later, among the Lisu here.

James little knew as he wrote those words just how fierce the battle was to be. 'I will not, by God's grace, let anything deter me.' This was the spirit in which he set out to survey the Upper Salween area of his field, and then settle among the Lisu to begin his work.

Black Lisu
On the journey to survey the Black Lisu country of the Salween gorges, James had Ba Thaw with him and also Mr Geis of the American Baptist Union, a man of about fifty and full of laughter and vitality. For two weeks they travelled through a 'wild, inhospitable region' northwards. They were making the journey in winter to avoid the rains this time, but the storms of high altitudes made the journey perilous. The following notes describe a little of it:

Spent the night on the top of a range ten thousand feet high, after two days with no human habitation. Darkness came on and snow began to fall. Our Lisu made a sort of booth for us. Morning, snow thick on the ground, obscuring the track. The Lisu, wet through, shivering with cold. Had to find our way over the pass. *K'u Teh liao-puh-teh* (extremity of suffering). Ba Thaw stubbed his foot, leaving blood marks all along the way. He had never been in snow before. No food till late in the afternoon when (below the snow line) we could make a fire. Saw armed robbers, but they did not attack us. Scenery magnificent. I enjoyed it after a fashion.

They had a new map of Yunnan with them this time, made by a Major Davies, and also a Royal Geographical Society report of the area. The road became a tiny track only inches wide in places, often making a mere ledge over a sheer drop of thousands of feet. Yet little Lisu log-cabins were perched wherever there was a water-supply. It was clear that there were tens of thousands of tribespeople in this area too.

Lonely Home

James made his home at Little River when the spring came, with Old Five as his faithful companion. 'A foaming river roars along two thousand feet below, and the mountains all around run up to over eleven thousand feet.' His room in this Lisu Hilton Hotel was, he felt, quite adequate.

It is really an out-house made of bamboos and thatch, all tumbling to pieces. But it has not come down on top of us yet. It leaks badly, but Old Five has patched it up by putting plantain leaves over the rotten roofing. The floor is as usual plain earth trodden hard, and there are a lot of old bins, baskets and things cumbering the ground. But such as it is I am very comfortable in it and do not hanker after anything better.

He had his Greek Testament and a few other books, a plate, a mug and some bedding. Rice and vegetables were provided by his host, and his 'bathroom' was a mere 2,000 feet below in the roaring torrent.

But as the days went by, James began to realize that he had appealed for prayer-partners none too soon. His need for this support was beginning to become acute. He had felt that the Lisu would soon be turning to Christ in large numbers. He had prayed, preached and taught, and God was now going to give the harvest.

But the Lisu were just not interested.

They were hospitable and they were friendly, but they were not interested in Jesus Christ.

Dark Shadow

A strange and sinister shadow fell over James's whole spiritual life. He was perplexed, and found himself in deepening gloom. At first he put it down to his isolation: a sense of loneliness engulfed him from time to time, but he knew it was not that. Then he wondered if it was the poor food: rice and vegetables made a seriously deficient diet (they laughed in Tengyueh when he once called in and consumed two tins of condensed milk straight off). But it was not the poor food; he was used to that. He looked out on the curtains of mist and rain and wondered if the depression was their doing. But gradually he became aware of an influence more far-reaching and soul-destroying than these physical discomforts.

He was assailed by deep and treacherous doubts. Yea, *hath* God said? The question came to him again and again, as clearly as it came at the dawn of time. Your prayers are not being answered, are they? No one wants to hear your message. The few who first believed have gone back, haven't they? You see, it doesn't work.

You should never have stayed in this area on such a fool's errand. You've been in China five years and there's not much to show for it, is there? You thought you were called to be a missionary. It was pure imagination. You'd better leave it all, go back and admit it was a big mistake.

Day after day and night after night he wrestled with doubt and suicidal despair. Suicidal? Not once, but several times he stared over the dark ravine into the abyss. Why not end it all?

The powers of darkness had him isolated; if they could get him now they could put an end to the work.

The rain fell steadily. The hut was becoming something of a quagmire even though Old Five repeatedly tried to stuff branches into the roof. But one day when the clouds were at their darkest, some letters arrived from Tengyueh, brought up the mountain by a weary, bedraggled runner.

One Magazine

James opened the letters carefully, lest he should tear the wet pages. One of the envelopes from England contained a copy of *The Overcomer*, a magazine he had not heard of before. He settled down to read it, rain dripping on all sides.

> I read it over and over — that number of *The Overcomer*. What it showed me was that deliverance from the power of the evil one comes through definite resistance on the ground of the Cross. I am an engineer and believe in things working. I want to see them work. I had found that much of the spiritual teaching one hears does not seem to work. My apprehension at any rate of other aspects of truth had broken down. The passive side of leaving everything to the Lord Jesus as our life, while blessedly true, was not all that was needed just then. Definite resistance

on the ground of the Cross was what brought me light. For I found that it worked. I felt like a man perishing of thirst, to whom some beautiful, clear cold water had begun to flow.

People will tell you, after a helpful meeting perhaps, that such and such a truth is the secret of victory. No: we need different truths at different times. 'Look to the Lord,' some will say. 'Resist the devil,' is also Scripture (James 4.7). And I found it worked! That cloud of depression dispersed. I found that I could have victory in the spiritual realm whenever I wanted it. The Lord Himself resisted the devil vocally: 'Get thee behind me, Satan!' I, in humble dependence on Him, did the same. I talked to Satan at that time, using the promises of Scripture as weapons. And they worked. Right then, the terrible oppression began to pass away. One had to learn, gradually, how to use the new-found weapon of resistance. I had so much to learn! It seemed as if God was saying: 'You are crying to me to do a big work among the Lisu; I am wanting to do a big work in you yourself.'

James was never able fully to put into words just how much that little magazine meant to him at that time. The long dark night in that poor hovel in the mountains ended in the dawn of victory. He was led in the *train of His triumph:* a triumph finished and complete.

The victory was, of course, a spiritual one. The outward circumstances were the same as before. The people of Little River were still not interested.

James pressed on with his study of the Lisu language, jotting down phrases and trying to invent a script of his own by manipulating the English alphabet to represent different sounds. In this he found children his best teachers: they loved to be with him, and never seemed tired of repeating phrases and tones for him.

Old Five Strangely

The enemy now reached for another weapon. Old Five
fell seriously ill. He lay in a delirious fever for several
days while James tended him and prayed for him,
concealing his fear of what the loss of his fellow-
worker might signify. Eventually Old Five's fever
subsided, but he was not fully delivered.

> It is painful for me to see him in this condition
> (James wrote to his mother). He has a peculiar
> expression at times, such as I have never seen in his
> sane moments — sometimes a worn harassed look,
> like a suffering old man, sometimes a dull, hard aspect
> of defiance. These uncanny moods of his are dis-
> tressing . . . He needs prayer, be sure of that — and I
> have not told you all that has been going on in my
> mind about this trouble.

It occurred to James now that Old Five was un-
likely to become the fellow-worker he had hoped for.
It was clear that all was not well in Old Five's life, and
two years after this he was excluded from the little
fellowship which had grown in his own village for
immorality. He was later restored, but although he
took part in the work again, he did not develop as
James's special partner.

When news came of the formation of a definite
prayer-circle in Letchworth it was an indescribable
joy. On his way to Tali, in the darkness and cold of a
leaky inn he wrote:

> When things seem to go wrong, I try to keep my
> mind in the attitude of Rom. 8.28, and my heart in
> the attitude of Phil 4.6, '— good wings on which to
> rise'! 'All things work together for good to them that
> love God' and 'In everything give thanks, for this is
> the will of God concerning you.'

Still Waters

It was a balm to James's heart to be able to spend some days at Tali with Mr Metcalf, who led the tribal work in the east of the province. Tali's blue lake stretches for thirty miles in length and six miles in breadth, running parallel to a range of snow-capped mountains rising to 14,000 feet. It was during the few days here that James found two Minchia women guides and scaled the highest peak, called the Tali mountain. It was quite an achievement; the 'Tali' defeated several expeditions of European climbers both before and after his ascent. From the walls of Tali city the Likiang peak could be seen on a clear day, the summit of which was 21,000 feet. He did not attempt this one! But he mentioned later (in 1937) that he saw many parties set out for it, none of whom succeeded.

Mr and Mrs Hanna provided generous hospitality and to James it seemed luxurious after his sojourn among the tribes. Best of all was the tuition under Mr Metcalf. James was able to learn much about missionary methods, language study and tribal church work from the experiences of this wise counsellor.

On his way back to Tengyueh he was encouraged to see the growth of the work in Paoshan, the city he had first visited five years previously. He stayed here for a month, the people crowding into the little shop he rented, until they overflowed into the street outside. It was not long after this that the believers built the first little chapel in that city, partly paid for by a gift from Letchworth. It was in the loving kindness of God that James saw such fruitfulness in the work just at this time. It was an oasis to a thirsty traveller.

A Loud Voice

Back in Tengyueh for a few days he prepared himself

for the next journey into the mountains. He was strengthened in body and in spirit. But he came briefly under another attack, the result of which is worth recording. He found his mind assailed by evil thoughts.

> These thoughts were present with me (he said himself) even when I was preaching. I went out of the city (Tengyueh) to a hidden gully on the hill-side, one of my prayer-haunts, and there voiced my determined resistance to Satan in the matter. I claimed deliverance on the ground of my Redeemer's victory on the Cross. I even shouted my resistance to Satan and all his thoughts. The obsession collapsed then and there, like a pack of cards, to return no more.
>
> James 4.7 is still in the Bible. Our Lord cried we are told 'with a loud voice' at the grave of Lazarus. He cried 'with a loud voice' from the Cross. In times of conflict I still find deliverance through repeating Scripture out loud, appropriate Scripture, brought to my mind through the Holy Spirit. It is like crashing through opposition. 'Resist the devil and he will flee from you.'

The Coolie Samaritan

It was about this time that a Burmese man, Mr Chang of Mahnyin, was visiting Tengyueh and saw something unusual on the road. A tall man dressed as a coolie was staggering under a heavy bundle on the approach road to the city. As Chang watched him pass he noticed he was a foreigner, and that the bundle was a Chinese coolie. It turned out that James had found a man dying at the side of the road and had carried him six miles on his back into the city. It was unusual behaviour in a land where every man generally fended for himself, and it was this roadside scene that began the chain of events which led Chang to Christ.

James was not regarded as particularly heroic by

most onlookers, however. Some Europeans, both missionary and otherwise, thought of him as an eccentric. Frank Dymond, whose own exploits as a Methodist missionary make stirring reading, remarked to his daughter one day that there was 'a strange chap who lives up in the mountains doing a kind of lone missionary work. No one seems to know much about him.'

A strange chap he must have seemed as he set out for Tantsah in the autumn of 1914. Not that he wanted to go alone, for he was companionable by nature, but he had to accept the fact that the burden he felt for the tribes of this area was a personal one. Besides, no one else could be spared to help him.

Tantsah Battleground

James had spent five weeks travelling around the villages of the Lisu and Kachin before deciding to settle at Tantsah. Everywhere the people in outlying areas said they would watch the attitude of the central places towards his message before deciding what theirs would be. So after careful prayer and thought he decided Tantsah was the most strategic place with forty villages immediately around it.

Winter was settling in as he arrived in Tantsah and it was already bitterly cold there, 6,000 feet above sea level. James found a two-roomed shack he could have as his home, and the forests supplied all the wood he needed for fuel. He wore Lisu clothes, ate Lisu food and now could converse fairly well in the Lisu language. His home he kept permanently open, and the people wandered in and out at will.

But the more he taught enquirers the more he felt the need for a written language., When they did become disciples of Christ, he thought, how could they follow Him if they couldn't read His commands? Besides, the people themselves would sit for long periods watching him write and sometimes trying to copy him. They badly wanted to read, too.

After some months, James felt that the interest shown by the people of Tantsah was growing. A good number came regularly to his little house to learn about the things of God. He felt it was time to go over into Burma and discuss the matter of Lisu writing with Mr Geis.

Before going, he gathered his friends together and asked them just how they felt about his teaching. Did they understand and accept that Jesus is the Son of God? He left them to talk it over among themselves. After some hours of parley they returned and said that they did accept his doctrines, and they wanted to become Christians if he would stay and teach them. They then joined him in a meal together as if to signify friendship towards him and his message.

Lisu Writing from Burma

At last the signs were encouraging, James felt, and a visit to Burma was warranted. He set off with high hopes, accompanied by a Mr Tsai who wanted to visit the Burmese markets. It was one of his happiest journeys. Approached from the Yunnan border, Burma looked unspeakably beautiful, and James wrote rapturous letters about the extensive forests and reflective glow of the Irrawaddy at Myitkyina. The help of Mr Geis and Ba Thaw with the formation of a Lisu script and a catechism provided enthralling hours. But underlying all this was the certainty of a great turning to Christ at Tantsah.

It was here in Burma that James came to a crisis in his apprehension of faith. Back in Tantsah it would have been easy to let the days go by in seeing to firewood, dealing with visitors and all manner of everyday affairs. But he had spent a good deal of time waiting on God. And in waiting, rather than calling, he had received a great deal in prayer.

Ever since his first meeting with Lisu tribesmen in the Tengyueh market place he had prayed for the tribespeople. He had been praying for a great turning to God among the Lisu for six years now. He had not minded hardship or privation in bringing the message; he had been willing to be purified and strengthened in the fire himself. But now, during his stay with Mr and Mrs Geis, he knew the Spirit of God was indicating that a new step must be taken. Ask in faith. He wrote to his prayer-partners:

> The Lord has taught me many things lately in regard to the spiritual life. In fact my own spiritual experience has undergone some upheavals during the past twelve months. Not the least important thing I have learned is in connection with the prayer of faith. I have come to see that in past years I have wasted much time over praying that was not effective prayer at all. Praying without faith is like trying to cut with a blunt knife — much labour expended to little purpose. For the work accomplished by labour in prayer depends on our faith: 'According to your faith,' not labour, 'be it unto you.'
>
> I have been impressed lately with the thought . . . that people fail in praying the prayer of faith because they do not believe that God *has* answered, but only that he *will* answer their petitions. They rise from their knees feeling that God will answer some time or other, but not that He has answered already. This is not the faith that makes prayer effective. True faith glories in the present tense, and does not trouble itself about the future. God's promises are in the present tense, and are quite secure enough to set our hearts at rest. Their full outworking is often in the future, but

God's word is as good as His bond and we need have
no anxiety. Sometimes He gives at once what we ask,
but more often He just gives His promise (Mark 11.24).
Perhaps He is more glorified in this latter case, for
it means that our faith is tried and strengthened. I
do earnestly covet a volume of prayer for my Lisu
work — but oh! for a volume of faith too. Will you
give this?

The sinews of his own faith were strengthening and
he felt the time had come for a definite prayer of faith
himself. It was at Mr Geis' house in Burma in 1915
that he made the transaction with God. He prayed a
clear and definite prayer, recorded in his diary and
in the annals of heaven, that God would bring several
hundreds of Lisu to saving faith in Him. It was a
prayer he had not prayed before and he never prayed it
again. It was not lightly done. Many years of preparation preceded this prayer, and James knew it was an
irrevocable step of faith.

I knew (he wrote not long after) that the time had
come for the prayer of faith. Fully conscious of what I
was doing and what it might cost me, I definitely
committed myself to this petition in faith (hundreds of
Lisu families for Christ). The transaction was done. I
rose from my knees with the deep restful conviction
that I had already received the answer.

Why 'Families'?

Perhaps you will wonder why I say families. It is
because only when the responsible members of any
particular family turn to God that the household
idolatrous implements may be removed, and until
that is done the real commitment has not been made.
A definite committal of some kind is of the first
importance among these people. If a man turns to
God but shrinks from burning the bridge behind him
by discarding his idolatrous utensils, he will as likely

as not slip back again into his old life. But if he once removes all idolatry from his home you may feel fairly certain of him afterwards. It is seldom that a man who takes this step reverts to demon-worship again; strong as is the hold demonolatry has upon the people, one such blow seems to break its power for ever. When these tribespeople turn to the Lord *en famille* it does not necessarily mean that every member of the family is wholehearted about the matter — indeed this is seldom the case — but it does mean that the responsible members of the family turn from Satan to God with a definiteness otherwise lacking. When, accordingly, I speak about so many Christian 'families', I mean families where those responsible have removed all vestige of demonolatry from the home. Much, of course, remains to be done after this, but you feel that you have, in a sense, already landed your fish when this step has been taken, and you thank God for the haul. In some cases a younger member of the family will turn Christian while the others hold back: he cannot then tamper with the household demonolatry. He may be quite sincere, and of course you receive him, but, as I say, such converts are apt to be unstable.

Opposition

James left Burma with peace of heart. But he had not gone far on his six-day journey back to Tantsah before messengers met him telling him there was trouble there. As he went on, more disturbing reports reached him until finally messengers arrived warning him that he should not go back at all.

He describes what he found when he reached Tantsah.

The very day I left for Burma the Chinese of Tantsah who outnumber the Lisu began to circulate wild stories about me . . . They said that I had come to the district with the intention of making it over to the British Government for money, and that Mr Tsai was my accomplice. Also that Tsai's going with me to

Myitkyina to buy salt was a blind; his real purpose
was to fetch the load of money the British Government was paying him! Some of them were for
confiscating his house and property right away.
Milder counsels however prevailed and they agreed to
wait until his return.

When he got back, they held what could only be
called an intimidation meeting. They summoned Tsai
and all the Lisu who had eaten the meal with me that
day . . . and after much argumentation made them
sign an agreement that they would on no account turn
Christian or allow me to come and live among them;
otherwise they would have their homes and property
confiscated. Tsai, as a kind of leader, was made to
stand the cost of a meal for all present. The Lisu,
overawed and alarmed, gave way entirely, and sent to
me, like the Gadarenes of old, and besought me 'to
depart from their borders' (Mark 5. 17).

James gathered his things from his little hut. At
least the Lisu felt as friendly as before, he noticed,
but they were too frightened to disobey the Chinese
majority. If he could get Government permission to
live there, they said, he would be welcome. It seemed
like the end of the work in Tantsah.

The true nature of his prayer of faith was now
clearly demonstrated.

If such a thing had happened a year ago (he wrote
to his Prayer Circle) it would have driven me down to
depths of depression. I have given way to discouragement, dark discouragement far too much in the past.
Now I know rather better, and thoroughly agree with
the assertion, 'all discouragement is of the devil'.
Discouragement is to be resisted just like sin. To give
way to the one is just as bad and weakens us as much
as to give way to the other. God has wonderfully
sustained me through this trial, and to Him be all the
praise when I say that not for one instant has it
disturbed my peace or radiant faith in the risen and

ascended Lord . . . God has enabled me to trust Him
more than ever before, to rejoice in Him more than
ever before, and to believe more than ever before for a
work of grace among the Lisu.

His wisest course now, he decided, would be to turn
south-west of Tengyueh into the mountains he had
first visited five years before. He talked to Mr and Mrs
Embery and they agreed that this area might well be a
fruitful one.

Six Week Tour

For six weeks he travelled from town to town and
village to village recording in his diary the adventures,
mishaps and encouragements, day by day. A spirit of
seeking impelled him on. Somewhere, sometime
God's word would yield a harvest. So he continued
preaching by the wayside, in the market place, under
the mid-day sun or by Lisu firesides at night. His diary
and his letters home are colourful and graphic.
'Preached by moonlight', he records, 'standing on a
big, high table in the street, with a smoky lantern.
Unusual attention.'

En route to a new settlement lay the small town of
Hsiangta. James reached it at nightfall, physically
very weary, and noticed that New Year festivities were
in full swing. He found somewhere to bed down for
the night — possibly in the open, as he frequently
did — and next morning felt a special need of spiritual
refreshment. He went out of the village.

Spent the day mostly in Bible reading and prayer,
alone on the mountains. Felt I needed it. Asked God to
give a blessing in the evening — my first visit to the
place. A stranger in a strange land, I knew no one at
all.

Pastrycook

Returning to the town, James found a theatrical company setting up their props in the market place. They had not begun their performance, so he struck up on his tiny accordion and began to sing. A crowd soon gathered and he started to explain the message he had come to bring. There were a few jeers and shouts of opposition from the back of the crowd, but about a hundred people stayed to listen until the moon was high. Before finishing James asked if any wanted to know more about Jesus Christ, the Saviour of the world.

A young man immediately stepped forward. He wanted to follow Jesus Christ, he said. He already believed He was the Son of God.

The man's name was Moh Ting-Chang, a pastry cook. He took James back to his little shop, and to his surprise Moh produced a small, well-read copy of Mark's gospel. Moh explained that his son had brought it back five years before after a visit to the Mangshi market, where a foreigner had given booklets out. Moh had read and re-read this little book many times. He was strangely stirred by the story. He had longed to learn more all these years. Wasn't Jesus truly God come into the world?

James and Moh were still talking as dawn filtered over the mountains. Moh wanted a week of questions answered, but James was expected up the valley later that day so he could not stay longer. He promised to be back within a few days.

After keeping his promised appointment up the valley, James hurried back to Moh. He was given a royal welcome. A bed was ready for him in a room above the shop; the best food prepared for him; Moh slept on the floor beside his bed to show him honour and respect. Even business was put aside so that Moh could spend every minute with his new friend.

After two days of discussion and going carefully through the catechism. James was convinced of the reality of Moh's conversion. The only thing that puzzled him as he sat in the room behind the shop was the large brass idol with the incense burning in front of it. After a few days he ventured to mention it. Oh, said Moh, he was afraid for his family if he touched that. Gently, James suggested that they should ask God about it. He was greatly moved to hear Moh's broken cry to God for strength to break with these things.

> When we rose from our knees he went straight to the stand where there was water and a basin, took a cloth and was about to approach the family altar, when again he hesitated.
> 'Come over here and let us pray once more,' I said, seeing the conflict.
> We did so and that settled it. Without a word he removed the strips of red paper with the characters for Heaven, Earth, etc., also the incense, paper-money and the idol. Without a word he burned them. I had never seen it done before in so summary a fashion. Later, Moh said more than once:
> 'If I have done right, I shall have good dreams to-night!'
> Needless to say, my first question in the morning was as to how he had slept.
> 'Good dreams, good dreams!' he answered heartily.
> And I could see that he was set at liberty.

News spread quickly that Moh had destroyed his idol and his symbols of ancestor worship. People came out curiously to see him stand with James as he preached.

'I never knew a braver man in his witness for Christ', James said later. 'Persecution assailed him from all sides . . . He has had his ups and downs but he has never denied his Lord.'

Salween and Mekong valleys

But there were other hamlets in the south-west area where there was some response to James's preaching. In some of the Lisu villages he was given a warm welcome and a ready hearing. The villagers loved to crowd round the evening fire and sing over and over again the songs he taught them and learn simple prayers. They told him there were many thousands of Lisu in the villages further south.

So for some weeks he set his face towards the vast ranges reaching down to Burma, Thailand and Vietnam, including the valleys carved out by the Salween and the Mekong rivers. There were a great many different tribes scattered on the fertile slopes never before visited by missionaries, and he had little idea of the harvest his early sowing was to produce. Doggedly he pressed on, up stony mountain trails and along the winding valley paths between village and village, looking everywhere for the spirit of enquiry that would mean God's time had come.

Upstairs room in Tantsah

Returning home after the long journey James heard that the opposition in Tantsah had died down and he was welcome there again. When spring came he was back there, this time installed in the rat-infested loft of the headman's house. His floorboards were loose and uneven, letting smoke and smells come up from down below; but they had the distinct advantage of allowing him also to hear all the chatter. It was useful language study. He joined the family for meals, a communal affair on the floor, surrounded by pigs, chickens and donkeys, looking out on the dark forests and the outlined peak of Clear Tooth standing up against the sky.

'Give me Lisu converts', he said as the summer came on, 'and I can truly say I will be happy in a pigsty.'

But he was beginning to realize the sinister nature of the evil powers in the area. Every inch of spiritual armour was needed to withstand it, and great strength 'having done all, to stand.' (Ephesians 6.13). His travels in the southern mountains had encouraged him, and he was increasingly thankful for the prayer companions in Letchworth, nine in all, who were going to pray him through. He wrote to each individually and, although letters took months to arrive, they each replied in person. It was a close relationship.

Sometimes he made the long journey on foot to Tengyueh, to make a break after months in the mountains. The Emberys and their children welcomed him as part of the family and shared in everything he had to tell.

They remembered later how James would arrive, dusty from his travels, and, after greeting them, make straight for the organ and pour out his soul in music, Bach, Beethoven, Schumann and Chopin, without a note in front of him, often for some hours. Even a cup of tea or a meal could not be pressed on him; this other hunger had to be satisfied. They remembered, too, how full of laughter the house was when he was with them. He had an infectious sense of the ludicrous, and a fund of anecdotes from his own adventures. To

James it was a much-needed rest from mountain living, and to be allowed to share in the Emberys' family life was almost like coming home.

The Weapon of All-Prayer

Back in Tantsah he was learning more and more that prayer was the only weapon that could drive back the forces of darkness. He had preached; he had taught; he had discussed; but there was little fruit. He wrote to his prayer-partners:

> About twelve men at Tantsah have professed their intention of being Christians. Of these, few or none come regularly to the services, nor do I know of any who have definitely renounced demonolatry — i.e. of those who are responsible members of their families. The 'strong man' has not yet been bound, if I may put it so. The majority of the people are too afraid of their demons to turn to God as yet. Still, God is leading me onward and I am quite hopeful. I do not intend to be in too much of a hurry, and yet I will cry to God for a blessed work of grace among the Lisu as long as He lends me breath.

Great were the strides in his understanding of prayer during these days. His own exercises in prayer gave him experience in the things of God, a knowledge of God; a friendship with God. His study of prayer in the Bible gave him a grasp of the whole vital subject in relation to the work of God. The Holy Spirit was opening up to him a whole new dimension of power through which he could become a prince with Him and prevail.

> 'If two of you', he wrote . . . 'shall agree . . .' I feel even when praying alone that there are two concerned in the prayer, God and myself . . . I do not think that a petition which misses the mind of God will ever be

answered (I John 5.14). Personally I feel the need of trusting Him to lead me in prayer as well as in other matters. I find it well to preface prayer not only by meditation but by the definite request that I may be directed into the channels of prayer to which the Holy Spirit is beckoning me. I also find it helpful to make a short list, like notes prepared for a sermon, before every season of prayer. The mind needs to be guided as well as the spirit attuned. I can thus get my thoughts in order, and having prepared my prayer can put the notes on the table or chair before me, kneel down and get down to business.

It was from Tantsah that James wrote the following letter to his praying friends, on October 9th 1915. He had a room to himself now, bare and dark with an earth floor and a rough table at which to write. The letter was taken by a Lisu runner to Tengyueh, a mountain journey of several days, and thence via Burma by sea to England, where it was kept and treasured by his praying band.

The Prayer of Faith

October 9, 1915

My dear Friends,
The Scriptures speak of several kinds of prayer. There is intercession and there is supplication, there is labour in prayer and there is the prayer of faith; all perhaps the same fundamentally, but they present various aspects of this great and wonderful theme. It would not be unprofitable to study the differences between these various scriptural terms . . .

Speaking generally, however, there is a distinction we all know; it is the distinction between *general* prayer and *definite* prayer. By definite prayer I mean prayer after the pattern of Matt. 21.21, 22; John 15.7; etc., where a definite petition is offered up and definite faith exercised for its fulfilment. Now faith must be exercised in the other kind of prayer also, when we

pray for many and varied things without knowing the
will of God in every case. I may pray much in this
general way, for instance, about the European War,
but I cannot offer much definite prayer, as I do not
know the purposes of God sufficiently well to do so.

In *general prayer* I am limited by my ignorance.
But this kind of prayer is the duty of us all (I
Timothy 2.1, 2) however vague it has to be. I may
know very little, in detail, about the object of my
prayer, but I can at any rate commend it to God and
leave it with Him. It is good and right to pray, vaguely,
for all people, all lands, all things, at all times. But
definite prayer is a very different matter. It is in a special
sense 'the prayer of faith.' A definite request is made in
definite faith for a definite answer. Let me pass on to
you a few thoughts that have been in my mind the last
few days on the subject of the **PRAYER OF FAITH**.

Take the case of a Canadian emigrant as an
illustration. Allured by the prospect of 'golden grain'
he leaves England for the Canadian West. He has a
definite object in his view. He knows very well what
he is going for, and that is wheat. He thinks of the
good crops he will reap and of the money they will
bring him:— much like the child of God who sets out
to pray the prayer of faith. He has his definite object
too. It may be the conversion of a son or daughter; it
may be power in Christian service; it may be guidance
in a perplexing situation, or a hundred and one other
things — but it is *definite*. To consider the points of
resemblance between the cases of the prospective
Canadian farmer and the believing Christian:

1. THE BREADTH OF THE TERRITORY
Think of the unlimited scope for the farmer in
Canada. There are literally millions of acres waiting
to be cultivated. No need, there, to tread on other
people's toes! Room for all — vast tracts of unoccupied land just going to waste and good land too.
And so it is with us, surely. There is a vast, vast field
for us to go up and claim in faith. There is enough
sin, enough sorrow, enough of the blighting influence

of Satan in the world to absorb all our prayers of faith, and a hundred times as many more. 'There remaineth yet very much land to be possessed.'

2. GOVERNMENT ENCOURAGES EMIGRATION

Think also of the efforts the Canadian Government are making to encourage emigration. All the unoccupied land belongs to it, but settlers are so badly needed that they are offered every inducement — emigration offices established, sea passages and railway fares reduced and grants of land made free! And God is no less urgently inviting His people to pray the prayer of faith; 'ASK, ASK, ASK,' He is continually saying to us. He offers his inducement too: 'Ask and ye shall receive, that your joy may be full.' All the unoccupied territory of faith belongs to Him. And He bids us to come and occupy freely. 'How long are ye slack to go in to possess the land?'

3. FIXED LIMITS

Yet this aspect of the truth must not be over-emphasized. Blessed fact though it be that the land is so broad, it can easily be magnified out of due proportion. The important thing is, not the vastness of the territory, but how much of it is actually assigned to us? The Canadian Government will make a grant of 160 acres to the farmer-emigrant, and no more. Why no more? Because they know very well that he cannot work any more. If they were to give him 160 square miles instead of 160 acres he would not know what to do with it all. So they wisely limit him to an amount of land equal to his resources.

And it is much the same with us when praying the prayer of definite faith. The very word 'definite' means 'with fixed limits.' We are often exhorted and with reason, to ask great things of God. Yet there is a balance in all things, and we may go too far in this direction. It is possible to 'bite off' even in prayer, 'more than we can chew.' There is a principle underlying 2 Cor. 10.13 which may apply to this very matter (see R.V. margin). Faith is like muscle which grows stronger and stronger with use, rather than indiarubber which can be stretched to almost any desired length. Overstrained faith is not pure faith, there is a mixture of the carnal element in it. There is no strain in the 'rest of faith.' It asks for definite blessing as God may lead; it does not hold back through carnal timidity, nor press ahead too far through carnal eagerness.

In my own case here (at Tantsah) I have definitely asked the Lord for several hundred families of Lisu believers. There are upwards of two thousand Lisu families in the district altogether. It might be said, 'Why do you not ask for a thousand?' I answer quite frankly, because I have not faith for a thousand. I have faith — or I would rather say, I believe the Lord has given me faith — for more than one hundred families but not for a thousand. So I accept the limits the Lord has, I believe, given me. Perhaps God will give me a thousand; perhaps too, He will lead me to commit myself to this definite prayer of faith later on. Someone has said that the Lord promises us bread, but he gives us bread and butter. This is in accordance with Eph. 3.20: 'Above all that we ask or think.' But we must not overload faith. We must be sane and practical. Let us not claim too little in faith, but let us not claim too much either. Remember the Canadian's 160 acres? Consider too how the Dominion Government exercises authority in the matter of location. The Government has a say as to the 'where' as well as the 'how much' of the emigrant's claim. He may not wander all over the prairie at his own sweet will, and elect to settle down in any place he chooses. Even in regard to the position of his farm, he must consult the Government.

Do we always do this in our prayers and claims? Do we consult the Heavenly Government at the outset, or do we pray 'the first thing that comes?' Do we spend much time waiting upon God to know His will, before attempting to embark on His promises? That is a principle upon which God works. He has informed us very plainly, in 1 John 5.14, 15. I cannot but feel that this is a cause (not the only cause) of many unanswered prayers. Jas. 4.3 has a broad application, and we need to search our hearts in its light. I read a testimony of Dr Stuart Holden's, not long ago, in which he said that one of the greatest blessings of his life had been his unanswered prayers. And I can say the same in my measure. Unanswered prayers have taught me to seek the Lord's will instead of my own. I suppose we have most of us had such experiences. We have prayed and prayed and prayed, and no answer has come. The heavens above us have been as brass. Yea, blessed brass, if it has taught us to sink a little more of this ever-present self of ours into the Cross of Christ. Sometimes our petition has been such a good one, to all appearances, but that does not ensure it being of God. Many 'good desires' proceed from our uncrucified selves. Scripture and experience certainly agree that those who live nearest to God are the most likely to know His will. We are called to be 'filled with the knowledge of His will' (Col. 1.9). The 'secret of the Lord is with them that fear Him; and He will show them His covenant.' We need to know more of the fellowship of Christ's death. We need to feed upon the Word of God more than we do. We need more holiness, more prayer. We shall not, then, be in so much danger of mistaking His will.

The wonderful promise of John 15.7 is prefixed by a far-reaching 'if'. I wonder if that verse might not be paraphrased: 'If ye abide NOT in Me and My words abide NOT in you, DO NOT ask whatsoever ye will for it shall NOT be done unto you.' Perhaps if we examined ourselves more thoroughly before God, we might even discover, in some cases, that the whole course of our life was not in accordance with His will. What right would a man have, in such a case, to expect his prayers to be answered? But is not this the fact with regard to much 'good Christian work?' 'Get your work from God' is a needed injunction. How often Christian leaders make their own plans, work hard at them, and then earnestly ask God's blessing on them. How much better, as Hudson Taylor felt, to wait on God to know His plans before commencing!

Much Christian work seems to have the stamp of the carnal upon it. It may be 'good', it may be successful outwardly — but the Shekinah Glory is not there.

Now all this applies to the prayer of faith. We must have the assurance that we are in the right place, doing the right work. We must be sure that God is leading us, when we enter upon specific prayer. It does not follow that because a thing is the will of God, He will necessarily lead *you* to pray for it. He may have other burdens for you. We must *get our prayers from God*, and pray to know His will. It may take time. God was dealing with Hudson Taylor for fifteen years before He laid upon him the burden of definite prayer for the foundation of the China Inland Mission. God is not in a hurry. He cannot do things with us until we are trained and ready for them. Let us 'press on' then (Phil. 3.12). We may be certain He has further service, further burdens of faith and prayer to give us when we are ready for them. And *He* will lead. Abraham would have never been a pattern of faith, if he had remained in Ur of the Chaldees. Nor will we ever have a faith worth calling faith unless we press forward in the footsteps of Him who said, 'Follow Me.'

4. THE CLAIM ENDORSED

Turn to the emigrant again. He has come to an agreement with the Canadian Government. He falls in with their terms; he accepts their conditions; he agrees to take over the land allotted to him. So he presents his claim at the proper quarter, and it is at once endorsed. Could anything be simpler? Nor need our claim in the presence of God be any less simple. When we once have the deep, calm assurance of His will in the matter, we put our claim, just as a child before his father. A simple request and nothing more. No cringing, no beseeching, no tears, no wrestling. No second asking either. The parable of the unjust judge was never meant to teach that we are to wring an answer by main force from an unwilling God. One real asking is enough for a life-time.

In my case, I prayed continually for the Tengyueh

Lisu for over four years, asking many times that several hundreds of families might be turned to God. This was only general prayer, however. God was dealing with me in the meantime. (Of course I do not mean to suggest that anyone else would necessarily be led along just the same line. Does God ever deal with two different people in exactly the same way?) Then near the end of November last year (1914), when staying with Mr and Mrs Geis down at Myitkyina in Burma, this same petition came to me as a definite burden. You know how a child is sometimes rebuked by his parents for asking something in the wrong way — perhaps in the case of a child, for asking rudely. The parent will say, 'Ask me properly.' That is just what God seemed to be saying to me then: 'Ask Me properly.' As much as to say, 'You have been asking Me to do this for the last four years without ever really believing that I would do it: now ask in FAITH.'

I recognised the burden clearly. And it was an actual burden: it *burdened* me. I went to my room alone one afternoon and knelt in prayer. I knew that the time had come for the prayer of faith. And then, fully knowing what I was doing and what it might cost me, I definitely committed myself to this petition *in faith*. I 'cast my burden upon the Lord'. I rose from my knees with the deep restful conviction that I had already received an answer. The transaction was done. And since then (nearly a year ago now) I have never had anything but peace and joy (when in touch with God) in holding to the ground already claimed and taken. I have never repeated the request and never will: there is no need. The asking, the taking and the receiving, occupy but a few moments (Mark 11.24). The past can never be undone, never need be redone. It is a solemn thing to enter into a faith-covenant with God. It is binding on both parties. You lift up your hand to God, perhaps even literally; you definitely ask for and definitely receive His proffered gift; then do not go back on your faith, even if you live to be a hundred.

5. GET TO WORK

To return once more to the Canadian farmer. He has put in his claim; the land has been granted; the deed made out and sealed with the Official seal. Is that the end then? No! only the beginning!

He has not attained his object yet. His object is a harvest of wheat, not a patch of waste land; and there is a vast difference between the two. The Government never promised him sacks of flour all ready for exportation — only the land which could be made to yield them. Now is the time for him to roll up his sleeves and get to work. He must build his homestead, **get his live-stock, call in labourers, clear the ground,** plough it and sow his seed. The Government says to him in effect, 'We have granted your claim: now go and work it.'

And this distinction is no less clear in the spiritual realm. God gives us the ground in answer to the prayer of faith, but not the harvest. That must be worked for in co-operation with Him. Faith must be followed up by works, prayer-works. Salvation is of grace but it must be worked out (Phil. 2.12) if it is to become ours. And the prayer of faith is just the same. It is given to us by free grace, but it will never be ours till we follow it up, work it out. 'Faith and Works' again. They must never be divorced; for indolence will reap no harvest in the spiritual world. I think the principle will be found to hold in any case where the prayer of faith is offered, but there is no doubt that it always holds good in cases where the strongholds of Satan are attacked, where the prey is to be wrested from the strong.

Think of the children of Israel under Joshua: God had given them the land of Canaan — given it to them (notice) by free grace — but see how they had to fight when once they commenced actually to take possession! Then again, think of Daniel (Daniel 10.12, 13): his prayer was answered the very first day he offered it; but that was only a signal for a twenty days' battle in the aerial heavens! Satan's tactics seem to be as follows. He will first of all oppose our breaking through to the place of real, living faith, by all means in his power. He detests the prayer of faith, for it is an authoritative 'notice to quit'. He does not so much mind rambling, carnal prayers, for they do not hurt him much. This is why it is so difficult to attain to a definite faith in God for a definite object. We often have to strive and wrestle in prayer (Eph. 6.10 etc.) before we attain this quiet, restful faith. And until we break right through and *join hands with God* we have not attained to real faith at all. Faith is a gift of God (Rom. 12.9); if we stop short of it we are using mere fleshly energy or will-power, weapons of no value in this warfare. However, once we attain to a real faith, all the forces of hell are impotent to annul it. What then? They retire and muster their forces on this plot of ground which God has pledged Himself to give us, and contest every inch of it. The real battle begins when the prayer of faith has been offered. But, praise the Lord! we are on the winning side. Let us read and re-read the tenth chapter of Joshua, and never talk about defeat again. Defeat, indeed! No, Victory! Victory! Victory!

2 Sam 23.8-23 is a passage along this line which has been meat and drink to me the last day or two. Verses 11 and 12 contain all I have been saying in a nut-shell. Please read them. Let Shammah represent the Christian warrior. Let David represent the crucified and risen Christ — and note that Shammah was 'one of the mighty men whom David had.' Let the 'plot of ground' represent the prayer of faith. Let the lentils, if you will, represent the poor lost souls of men. Let the Philistines represent the aerial hosts of wickedness. Let 'the people' represent Christians (maybe good people) afflicted with spiritual anaemia. I can imagine what these people were saying as they saw the Philistines approaching and ran away:

'Perhaps it was not the Lord's will to grant us that plot of ground. We must submit to the will of God.'

Yes, we must indeed submit ourselves to the will of God, but we must 'resist the devil' too (Jas 4.7.) The fact that the enemy comes upon us in force is no proof

that we are out of the line of God's will. The constant
prefixing of 'if it be Thy will' to our prayers is often a
mere subterfuge of unbelief. True submission to God
is not inconsistent with virility and boldness. Notice
what Shammah did — simply *held his ground*. He
was not seeking more worlds to conquer at that
moment! He just stood where he was and hit out,
right and left. Notice also the result of his action and
to whom the glory is ascribed!

6.   PRAYING THROUGH TO VICTORY

I repeat that this does not necessarily apply to every
kind of prayer. A young Lisu Christian here is fond of
telling an experience of his a few months ago. He was
walking through the fields in the evening when his
inside began to unaccountably pain him. He dropped
on his knees and, bowing his head down to the
ground, asked Jesus to cure him. At once the stomach-
ache left him. Praise the Lord! And there are no doubt
multitudes of such cases — simple faith and simple
answers. But we must not rest content with such
prayer. We must get beyond stomach-ache or any
other ache, and enter into the deeper fellowship of
God's purposes. 'That ye be no longer children'
(Eph. 4.14). We must press on to maturity. We must
attain to 'the measure of the stature of the fulness of
Christ,' and not remain in God's kindergarten indefinitely. If we grow into manhood in the spiritual
life we shall not escape conflict. As long as Eph. 6.
10-18 remains in the Bible, we must be prepared for
serious warfare — 'And having done all, to stand.' We
must fight through, and then stand victorious on the
battle-field.

Is not this the secret of many unanswered prayers
— that they are not fought through? If the result is not
seen as soon as expected, Christians are apt to lose
heart, and if it is still longer delayed, to abandon it
altogether. You know the name they give to places in
England when the building (or whatever it is) is
abandoned when only half completed — So and so's
'Folly'. I wonder whether some of our prayers do not

deserve the same stigma. Think of Wembley Tower: I
have never examined it closely, but from a distance it
looks as if a good beginning had been made. Luke
14.28-30 applies to prayers as well as towers. We must
count the cost before praying the prayer of faith. We
must be willing to pay the price. We must mean
business. We must set ourselves to 'see things through'
(Eph. 6.18, 'In all perseverence'). Our natural strength
will fail: and herein lies the necessity for a divinely-
given faith. We can then rest back in the Everlasting
Arms and renew our strength continually. We can
then rest as well as wrestle. In this conflict-prayer,
after the definite exercise of faith, there is no need to
ask the same thing again and again. It seems to me
inconsistent to do so. Under these circumstances, I
would say let prayer take the following forms:

(a) A firm *standing on God-given ground,* and a
constant assertion of faith and claiming of victory. It
is helpful, I find, to repeat passages of Scripture
applicable to the subject. Let faith be continually
strengthened and fed from its proper source — the
Word of God.

(b) A definite fighting and *resisting of Satan's host*
in the Name of Christ. I like to read passages of
Scripture, such as 1 John 3.8, or Rev. 12.11 in prayer,
as direct weapons against Satan. I often find it a
means of much added strength and liberty in prayer to
fight this way. Nothing cuts like the word of the
Living God. (Eph. 6.17, Heb. 4.12).

(c) *Praying through* every aspect of the matter in
detail. In the case of my Lisu work here, I continually
pray to God to give me fresh knowledge of His will,
more wisdom in dealing with the people, knowledge
of how to pray, how to maintain victory, how to
instruct people in the gospel, or in singing or in
prayer, help in studying the language, help in
ordinary conversation, help in preaching, guidance as
to settling down somewhere as a centre, guidance
about building a house (if necessary), guidance as
regards my own arrangements (servants, money, food,
clothes, etc.) help and blessing in my correspondence,

opening for the Word and blessing in other villages, for leaders and helpers to be raised up for me, for each of the Christians by name, also for every one of my prayer helpers by name. Such detailed prayer is exhausting, but I believe effectual in regard to ascertaining the will of God and obtaining His highest blessing.

I would not ask anyone to join me in the definite prayer for the turning to God of several hundred Lisu families, unless God gives individual guidance to do so. Better offer prayer in a more general way than make a definite petition apart from His leading. I should, however, value highly the prayer-co-operation of any who felt led to join me in it. What I want too, is not just an occasional mention of my work and its needs before the Lord, during the morning or evening devotions, but a definite time (say half an hour or so?) set apart for the purpose every day, either during the day-time or in the evening. Can you give that time to me — or rather to the Lord?

About a fortnight ago I baptized two Lisu women at the little village of Six Family Hollow — the wives of the two young Lisu men I baptized last January. I have now baptized six Christian Lisu altogether, all from that one family. It was my painful duty only the next day, however, to exclude one of these, a man named Ahdo, from church fellowship, for an indefinite period. He is the man who first introduced me to the Lisu in his home and in many of the surrounding villages, and until the end of last year, he acted as my preacher and 'helper' when with me. It appears that he has been continually, during the past few years and until now, not only in his own village but in other places where he has been with me, breaking the seventh commandment. The Lisu are a very immoral race in any case, but in spite of his Christian profession, he has been even more sinful than most of them. Such things will go on sometimes almost indefinitely, no one but the foreign missionary being ignorant of them. I had baptized him with his younger brother and both parents last January, but he had not been with me since then. I am glad to say, however, that he seems quite penitent and never attempted to deny it. We must pray for his restoration. I have no other special news of the work, just now. I am thinking of visiting that village (Six Family Hollow) again in a few days, as well as other villages.

Hoping to write again next month and with earnest prayers for you all,

Yours in the Lord's service,
J. O. Fraser.

5   MOUNTAIN RAIN

Break in the Clouds

The old man was angry with the spirits. Groping round his darkened room he cursed the demon priest and the path to his house. The pain in his eyes was scarcely bearable and his wife and children kept their distance, silently chopping pine chips below the oak stump. Pain was making Old Fish dangerously bold, they thought, bolstered no doubt by their neighbour, old Mrs Tsai, who broke with the spirits years ago.

Finally the old man, shielding his eyes from the sun, stumbled down to them. They had long talked about Mrs Tsai's God. The spirits were an expensive waste of time. Might Mrs Tsai have found the truth?

> He actually took a sword, (James wrote) and chopped down his family altar, refusing to burn any incense or paper money, though it was the Chinese New Year. He had heard the Gospel previously, but this is the first case I have come across of a man definitely discarding idolatry on his own initiative. I did not visit him till nearly three months after that, during which time he had gone down to my colleague, Mr Embery, and obtained some eye-lotion, and was quite relieved of the pain. I stayed three days in his home, and found him, and his wife and children, as well as his old father and mother, singularly wholehearted in their determination to worship God.
>
> This case has been noised abroad throughout the district and has made a favourable impression. The only thing many of the people are waiting for is to

know whether it is really safe to throw the evil spirits overboard and turn to Christ. It is important to pray for those who have already turned Christian, that their faith and constancy may be equal to all tests and that the Spirit's power for the healing of sickness may be with them. For a man to turn Christian and then be smitten down with sickness, at once discredits the Gospel in the eyes of the Lisu.

Mother Tsai was the spiritual rock of her family, unshaken by opposition and family problems. Her faith was childlike and strong. Three times, she assured James, her pig had run away and each time she found it after prayer. Infant faith for infant prayer, but with it the dawning understanding of a covenant-keeping God.

Here and there, then, tiny lights shone out in the spiritual darkness of the area. But generally the clouds were as black as ever. James needed vigilance to keep the gloom from settling again over his own soul. The hardest tests were the plain setbacks. Families seemed to accept the message readily, even acknowledge Jesus as Lord, and then fall away again. It was Satan's war of attrition.

The next few months chronicled the journey of a soul. Waiting week after week for the turning to God he had prayed for, and seeing nothing, James found the battle was not only against the prince of the mountains. It was in himself.

'What was your biggest surprise when you went to China?' asked a student, eagerly looking at a veteran missionary.

'Myself,' he replied.

The Sword-Ladder
There were times when James's faith in the power of the Cross itself was tested as when he saw how deeply

soaked in demonism the people were. He had high
hopes of some enquirers near Tantsah at first. They
had shown a lively interest. They lived near Cold
Horse Village and the demon priest there didn't mind
if James taught the people. The priest, who said that
he himself was 'possessed by spirits and belonged to
them,' invited him to the next Sword Ladder Festival
where there would be hundreds of people. He agreed
to come thinking he would get a large audience.

It happened that a missionary by the name of Goby
was visiting James at the time, so they went together
and wandered about among the crowds. He wrote
about it in a letter home.

> The sword-ladder had about three dozen rungs and
> was fixed vertically. It stood right out in an open place
> and was some forty feet high. The evening before the
> ascent, the 'devil-dancer', a man of over sixty years of
> age, was supposed to 'wash' his hands and feet in a fire
> of red-hot cinders. Goby and I went to the temple
> to witness this. There was a whole lot going on.
> Sacrifices were being offered to some hideous looking
> idols, including one or two chickens which the devil-
> dancer killed by biting through their necks with his
> own teeth . . . With the beating of drums and gongs,
> they were trying to work up some kind of frenzy, but
> with only partial success. At length the devil-dancer
> emerged from the temple and just swept the red-hot
> coals about with his bare hands and feet . . . We both
> noticed, next day, that his hands showed signs of
> being burnt.
>
> The old devil-dancer did not emerge from the
> temple till about 2 p.m. (next day) and, after more
> incantations, proceeded very slowly to ascend the
> ladder. After more talk and carrying-on at the top, he
> slowly came down again. Then two others, younger
> men, went up and down again. A woman also very
> nearly did so. She has, as they say, fits of demon-
> possession in her home, and was to be cured by

mounting the ladder of knives through the power of her 'god'. But she, apparently, could not get hold of the inspiration necessary, so after carrying on in a wild kind of way for a while, she gave up the attempt.

Fear was written on the faces of the crowd. They didn't enjoy it. It simply proved again to James that these people were children of darkness, born and bred. They had to perform these rituals and had to obey the spirits, exercising no will of their own in the matter at all.

Even those who had seemed interested now fell away. Total darkness surged back.

> I was very severely disappointed (he wrote) about the attitude of the Lisu of that district, to the Gospel. They received the Word with joy at first, as they so often do. Several announced that they were going to turn Christian; one old man and his son seemed specially earnest. Then the spirit of fear seemed to possess them, and one by one they dropped off, until no one would take a stand at all. We had to leave them as heathen as I first found them. It was a very painful experience and seemed almost to stun me for awhile.

Numb and wounded, James took up arms again. 'Rejoice not against me, O mine enemy. When I fall I shall arise' (Micah 7.8).

> Quite crushed with sorrow for a while whence an effort helped me, outside the village — a straight-out, right-from-the-shoulder prayer against Satan restored faith and peace. The spirit of depression had to be entirely driven away, for victory.

Suffering in Prayer
For some days after this James studied the relationship between desire and prayer. Goby had travelled on, so he was alone.

He was consumed with desire to see a work of God among the Lisu; a passionate, even desperate wanting filled him when he turned to prayer. It was as if God had shown him something of the unfathomable longing of His own Spirit. And just as he shared fellowship with the Spirit in this agony of desire, he wanted his prayer-partners to suffer in the same way.

He wrote to them about Hannah in I Samuel 1.

> How much of our prayer is of the quality we find in this woman's 'bitterness of soul', when she 'prayed unto the Lord'? How many times have we ever 'wept sore' before the Lord? . . . We have prayed much, perhaps, but our longings have not been deep as compared with hers. We have spent much time upon our knees, it may be, without our hearts going out in an agony of desire. But real supplication is the child of heartfelt desire, and cannot prevail without it; a desire not of earth nor issuing from our own sinful hearts, but wrought into us by God Himself. Oh, for such desires! Oh, for Hannah's earnestness, not in myself only but in all who are joining me in prayer for these poor heathen aborigines!
>
> And is there not sufficient reason for such earnestness? We have our Peninnahs as surely as ever Hannah had and as God's saints have had all down the ages. David's eyes ran down with rivers of water, because the ungodly observed not God's law (Ps. 119. 136). Jeremiah wept with bitter lamentation, because of the destruction of the holy city. Nehemiah fasted, mourned and wept when he heard of the fresh calamities which had befallen Jerusalem. Our Lord wept over it, because of its hardness of heart. The Apostle Paul had 'great sorrow and unceasing pain' in his heart on account of his brethren according to the flesh (Rom. 9.2).
>
> Yes, and we have our 'sore provocations', or should have. How else ought we to feel when we see all the ungodliness and unbelief round us on every hand. Would a light-hearted apathy become us under such

circumstances? No, indeed! And I want you, please, to join me — or rather, share with me — in the provocation which is daily with me in my work among the Lisu. Let the terrible power of evil spirits among them be a provocation to you. Let their sinfulness, their fears, their pitiful weakness and instability be a provocation to you. Ask God to lay the burden upon you, and that heavily . . . that it may press you down upon your knees. My prayer for you is that God will work such sorrow within you that you will have no alternative but to pray. I want you to be 'sore provoked' as I am.

Such a state of mind and heart is only of avail, however, as it is turned into prayer. Desire, however deep, does nothing in itself, any more than steam pressure in a boiler is of use, unless it is allowed to drive machinery. There is a spiritual law here. A strong spiritual desire does harm rather than good, if it is neglected . . . An earnest desire in spiritual things is a bell ringing for prayer. Not that we should wait for such desires . . . We should pray at all seasons, whether we are prayer hungry or not. If we have a healthy prayer-appetite, so much the better; but if this appetite be unnoticed or unappeased, a dullness will come back over us and we shall be weakened in spirit, just as lack of sufficient food weakens us in body. See, in I Sam. 1.15, the way in which Hannah dealt with her God-given desire. Her soul was bitter, and she 'poured it out' before the Lord. Blessed bitterness! but it must be poured out.

It would be difficult to put into words just how much the prayer-circle meant to James during the next five months at Tantsah. There was virtually nothing to show for his labours; no turning: little response. His endless tramping around the mountains appeared more or less fruitless.

He had eight or ten people in his treasured prayer-band. It needed perseverance to pray for a lone and distant missionary working with so little success.

Besides, letters were very out of date by the time they came with news. They took at least six weeks. But now James wrote and asked for reinforcements.

> I am persuaded that England is rich in godly, quiet, praying people, in every denomination. They may not be a great multitude as far as numbers are concerned, but they are 'rich in faith', even if many of them be poor and of humble station. It is the prayers of such that I covet more than gold of Ophir — those good old men and good old women (yes, and not necessarily old either) who know what it is to have power with God and prevail . . . Will you help me, prayerfully and judiciously, to get some of these to join the circle? . . . The work for which I am asking prayer is the preaching and teaching the Word of God, pure and simple . . . I have no confidence in anything but the Gospel of Calvary to uplift these needy people.

He needed prayer himself. He was aware of defeats inside: discouragement, listlessness and impatience. He recorded in his Journal many aspects of the long battle of these days. It is the story of a spiritual travail, and without it a work of God is not brought to birth. It is a very human story, too, of defeat and humiliation as well as muscular faith.

Daily Testing

The trials of everyday life were a test in themselves. The bitter winds of winter gave way to the steady, grey rain of the spring. His bare quarters seemed permanently damp. Now and then he was simply tired of the dirt. It was not just the mud and the result of Lisu spitting everywhere, but having his bedding infested with lice and bedbugs that irritated. And after several months of a rice diet his whole body craved a change of food: something sweet, or some butter and cheese.

His legs were still swollen from earlier travels and he usually had to bind them up before getting off his mattress in the morning to relieve the varicose ulcers.

After some of his journeys on foot around the mountain villages every bone seemed to be aching and every muscle stiff. Who was to know, anyway, if he lay in bed half the day?

January 1, 1916. Must watch against getting up too late, these intensely cold mornings. The indwelling Christ is my successful weapon against all sin these days — praise Him!

Sunday, January 2 . . . An earnest desire to save souls is on me, but prayer is rather unstable. I must regain my equilibrium in the prayer life. I must maintain, also, my abiding in Christ, by prayer without ceasing (silent), which I am now finding blessedly possible. Romans 6 is not now my weapon, so much as John 15.

Tuesday, January 4. Finished Finney's Autobiography: much help received from it. Finney's strong point is the using of means to an end. My own leading is not a little along that line also. I do not intend to be one of those who bemoan little results, while 'resting in the faithfulness of God'. My cue is to take hold of the faithfulness of God and USE THE MEANS necessary to secure big results.

Saturday, January 8. Prayer out on the hill, from noon till about 3.30 p.m. Much drawn out for Lisu work generally.

Sunday, January 9. Discussion with Ku's family about his removing the 'family altar' as well as the betrothal ceremony of his son, to-morrow.

Monday, January 10 . . . Nearly all the Christians away at Ku's betrothal ceremony (where there would be drinking and dancing etc.). I spent most of the evening in prayer. Nothing will give me lasting joy on this earth, now, but the salvation of large numbers of Lisu. To hear of Lisu 'turning' anywhere, or even intending to turn, rejoices me in a way that nothing else does.

Sunday, January 16. Not a single one to Service in the morning . . . The walls of Jericho fell down 'by faith' (not the faith of the walls, though!). Of all the instances of faith in Hebrews, this corresponds most nearly to my case. But not faith only was necessary; the wall fell down after it had been compassed about for seven days. Seven days' patience was required . . . and diligent compassing of the city every day too — which seems to typify encompassing the situation by regular systematic prayer. Here then we see God's way of success in our work, whatever it may be — a trinity of prayer, faith and patience.

Tuesday, January 18. Prayer, to-day, rather on general than particular lines; patience the chief thought. Abraham was called out by God and went in blind faith; when he got to the land of promise, he found nothing but a famine — much like me with the Lisu, these two years. But Abraham, or his seed, possessed the milk and honey of the whole land, later on. God's time had come for Abraham, but not for the Amorites. God's time has come for me, but not, perhaps, just this month or this year, for the Lisu.

Am impressed, too, that I do not yet know the channels which the grace of God is going to cut out among the people here. Hence general prayer has its place, until God's plan is revealed a little more fully.

Secret Commitment

One of James's helpers these days was bad-tempered and often rude. He wasted James's time and money and seemed incapable of doing a job properly. James nearly met his Waterloo over this at the time. It was a battle to control a 'fierce impatience' that welled up inside him. He was deeply troubled at his own spirit. It wasn't that he couldn't keep cool outwardly, but that he felt so angry inwardly: this was the defeat. He knew absolutely that Jesus promised deliverance from this very thing, and that his 'spirit, soul and body could be preserved blameless.' (I Thess. 5.23). He was reading S.D. Gordon's *Wilderness Conflict* at the time, and quotes from it in his journal. 'I do not mean ask God to give you victory', he quoted, 'plead less, and claim more, on the ground of the blood of Jesus Christ.'

Only the eyes of God could see the secret striving of a man whose ambition was to stand complete in Him. There was no one else there to see.

'From long experience and observation', wrote John Wesley, 'I am inclined to think that whoever finds redemption in the blood of Jesus — whoever is justified — has the choice of walking in the higher or lower path. I believe the Holy Spirit at that time sets before him "the more excellent way" . . . to aspire after the heights and depths of holiness — the entire image of God. But if he do not accept this offer, he insensibly declines into the lower order of Christians . . .'

James's reading and the accounts in his Journal show the set of his face from the lower slopes towards the summit. His diary was honest in its account of the battles.

Tuesday, February 1. Prayer in the afternoon for about three hours, but not enough grip or intelligent method — as if I have arrears of prayer to make up.

Thursday, February 3. Depressed after defeat this morning, from which no real recovery all day (last day of the Chinese year).

Friday, February 4. No meal till 2 p.m. Thoroughly depressed about state of work in Tantsah. No one to count upon in matters demanding an earnest spirit . . . The evil one seems to have the upper hand in me to-day as well as in the Christians. Fighting between Gu and Ku in the evening, also between Adu and O.S. Ku off to the dances. Several visitors during the day . . . A little prayer in much distress of soul, on top of hill. Feel much inclined to 'let Ephraim alone' . . . But just

here I am torn between two alternatives — for I seem
to have no leading to leave Tantsah, any more than
the Lord had to leave Jerusalem (Luke 19.41) . . . My
prayer is not so much, 'Lord, lead me somewhere else',
as 'Lord, give me a solid church, here in Tantsah'.

Saturday, February 5th. Yesterday's attack of depression and defeat almost got over, but not quite.
Such times are not easy to recover from, I find.
Enabled in large measure, however, to adopt the
attitude of combined common-sense and restful faith.
The two O.S.'s came in this evening, with whom
useful talk, as also with Ku. Still much distressed,
however, over the condition of things . . . The
majority of Christians have gone in for whisky-
drinking . . . The outlook here in Tantsah at present
seems less hopeful than at any time since I first set foot
in the place.

I am not, however, taking the black, despondent
view I took yesterday . . . the opposition will not be
overcome by reasoning or by pleading, but by (chiefly)
steady, persistent prayer. The men need not be dealt
with (it is a heart-breaking job, trying to deal with a
Lisu possessed by a spirit of fear) but the powers of
darkness need to be fought. I am now setting my face
like a flint: if the work seems to fail, then *pray;* if
services etc., fall flat, then *pray still more;* if months
slip by with little or no result, then *pray still more and
get others to help you.*

Sunday, February 6 . . . B. and Va announce that
they will become Christians, if their parents will allow
them . . . Four young men say they will follow Christ,
whatever happens . . . I adopt an entirely new attitude
with them for the first time, concealing my earnest
desire beneath a calm, almost indifferent exterior. I
now think that this is the best way after all . . . It will
give them more confidence.

Tuesday, February 8. Mo La P' turns Christian in
the morning. Gu, Va and T, all at his house . . . Full of
joy and praise.

Family Bonfires

There were moments of joy in these days too: little

encouragements, that he might not be tried beyond his endurance.

On his travel to a southward village, James stayed in what he called a Black Hole of Calcutta house, and as he prepared to set off in the morning the villagers gathered round him and begged him to stay: they wanted to become Christians.

After much explaining and teaching, he prayed with them and then stood and watched as they tore down the objects of demon-worship. 'We had a fine old blaze', he wrote. 'The joy of seeing this done is second only to the joy of baptizing.'

A family in a nearby village followed suit, and after their bonfire even led James round the house, both inside and out 'to check if it was all O.K.' he records. Different spirits operated inside and outside the house, they believed, and they wanted to make a clean sweep of them all.

The Crucial Conflict
But there were times of inward defeat. There was no local fellowship to undergird his faith, and no partner to pray with. In his solitary room James came to understand that if he caved in spiritually now, there was no future for the work. He wrote in March:

> The question now remains whether I intend really to consecrate myself to the Lord, or to compromise.
> Last night's compromise continued until this morning, with distressing turmoil in consequence. Not enabled to take the crucified position till mid-day. A wasted morning as a natural result . . . Oh, I am myself needing far, far more prayer these days!

Two days later he was writing with reference to one who was causing anxiety:

O Lo Si here in the evening . . . After he left, was enabled to strive for him in prayer, with the result that I now hear of his re-decision to be a Christian. He must be held on to in faith, however. Much helped by Mrs Penn-Lewis's bringing out the point 'SAY to this mountain'. Was enabled to *say,* this evening. Retired, strong in spirit.

Someone was still sending him copies of *The Overcomer* magazine, and he was greatly strengthened by its articles, often by Jessie Penn-Lewis. Years later a friend expressed some surprise when James mentioned this.

'I don't find her articles at all helpful', she commented. 'She seems too preoccupied with the devil.'

James turned to her. 'The need is the key', he answered.

No one travels far on his spiritual pilgrimage without an encounter with the enemy, and the enemy knows a strategic target. Out of the conflict of these days some of James's best writings emerged. New light came to him on the nature of spiritual warfare. The strong take the kingdom of heaven by force. (Matt. 11.12).

March 20. Each time your spirit goes under and faints in the testing and trials which come to you, you lose mastery over the powers of darkness, i.e. you get below them instead of abiding above them in God. Every time you take the earth standpoint — think as men think, talk as men talk, look as men look — you take a place below the powers of darkness. The mastery of them depends upon your spirit abiding in the place above them, and the place above them means knowing God's outlook, God's view, God's thought, God's plan, God's ways, by abiding with Christ in God.

You may be so entangled in the things of earth that

your spirit cannot rise above them. The devil knows this and pours earthly things upon you to keep you down, so that you go under and not over when the battle comes.

Rom. 8.11. You must know the quickening of the body to a very great extent if you are to be able to endure the conflicts of this present hour. Your natural strength would go under, so God 'quickens your mortal body' to make you able to endure what no flesh and blood could endure and live. One of the temptations in the spirit-warfare is when your body begins to flag, to say, 'I must give up', instead of casting yourself upon 'God that raises the dead' and can quicken the mortal body to endure and triumph in and through all things.

Eph. 6.10. Oh how we need STRENGTH, for often we can hardly hold our ground!

In every battle there are crucial spots. Get near and stay near to your Divine Chief until He turns and points them out. And at those points face and force the fight. And though the conflict be keen, though defeat seems certain, though the battle should continue for hours, for days, for months, even for years, yet hold on, HOLD ON; for to such Jer. 1.19 is written: 'They shall fight against thee but they shall not prevail against thee, for I am with thee to deliver thee.'

The aim of Satanic power is to cut off communication with God. To accomplish this aim he deludes the soul with a sense of defeat, covers him with a thick cloud of darkness, depresses and oppresses the spirit, which in turn hinders prayer and leads to unbelief — thus destroying all power (instead of seeing Heb. 11.1).

Any position you have really taken with God's help, may be re-taken at once by faith after a temporary lapse.

It is one of the most subtle wiles of the foe to get us occupied with superficial and surface concerns (e.g. book-selling, language study, running mission-stations, report-writing, correspondence, account-keeping, building, repairs, buying things, reading,

etc., etc.) The enemy is delighted to have us so
occupied incessantly with secondary and trival
concerns as to keep us from attacking and resisting in
the true spirit of the conflict. WEIGH THESE
WORDS. J.O.F.

Some days James felt spiritually strong and able to
stand his ground against the odds. At other times he
felt lethargic and weak, as if his feet were slipping.

One day he had weakened in prayer and allowed his
thoughts to wander. It had been a day of defeat in
general. When three of his most promising enquirers
came for the evening Bible Study James tells what
happened.

> A very definite sense of spiritual weakness —
> aggravated, no doubt, by further defeat in the evening
> with Ku, Va and O.S. The latter seemed almost as if
> possessed by a laughing demon, so entirely foreign to
> his usual demeanour! Insane giggling during study,
> followed by a burst of laughter (the first I remember
> here, from any Christian) as soon as I commenced to
> pray. Va follows him, more or less. I stop praying and
> burst out at him in carnal anger which quite fails,
> from almost every point of view. But I feel quite
> incompetent to deal with it; unequal to the situation;
> master neither of myself nor anyone else. Feel weak,
> lazy and semipassive; have lost my grasp of things.
> O.S.'s unnatural flippancy seems only a reflection of
> my own condition. Almost feel as if a demon were
> laughing at me through him because of my powerless-
> ness, defeat and spiritual inertia.
>   REFUSE, however, to be discouraged, but get
> down on my knees at once and 'get right with God'. I
> have had many such experiences (failures) before, but
> have made the mistake of giving way to depression
> instead of calmly investigating the cause of things.
> This time, however, the thief is not going to escape . . .
>   Formerly it used to take me days to recover from
> such defeat. Then, when I began to know better, it

took a few hours. But now I know even that to be too long, and only allow a few minutes for complete recovery. The sooner the better, and there is no time limit. (I John 1.9).

Sound in Mind

A healthy sense of balance shows itself here in the pages of his diary. It isn't good to sit for long hours in a dark room. Up and out, he told himself. Go for a walk. Take a book into the sunshine and do some language study.

'Sometimes', he wrote, 'a general state of defeat and weakness is cured as if by magic by setting to and doing some honest work'.

The dark little shanty had closed in on him too much, and he now felt it was high time to get up and out and sing praise to God for the victory won among the armies of heaven.

Yes, PASSIVITY, or call it by an uglier word, LAZINESS is the cause of half my defeat. I need never be defeated, as I know quite well. Victory all the rest of the day. This bears out what I have been learning . . . When you are weak and feel unable to free yourself from the power of sin — just up and sing a song, or shout a determined note of defiance against the enemy; then roll up your sleeves and do some good Lisu study. Lack of this spirit brings defeat. Moral:

TRY TO FIND GOD'S BALANCE BETWEEN PRAYER AND WORK.

Oh yes, we Christians need never be overcome! One weapon at least will always be found to work, if others fail . . . When we are defeated there is a cause. We should not pass it over as inexplicable. Cast about to find the cause with the help of the Holy Spirit. Then put the thing away, and avoid it in the future . . .

Spent most of the morning in prayer, very peace-

fully — drawn out especially for O Lo Si, or against
the powers of darkness, rather, that hold him back.
This prayer continued in power until, apparently,
fought right through . . . Rest of the day in Lisu study,
thoroughly wholesome. Friday's lesson is being still
further burnt into me. Yes, God teaches all right.

He had felt 'drawn out' in prayer for O Lo Si, and
'fought right through' for him, conscious of a power
working through him. Within two or three weeks he
wrote:

To-day saw the biggest victory since ever I set foot
in Tantsah. O Lo Si's demonolatry came down. Ku S.
very helpful . . . Oh, to learn more about co-operation
with God in all things! This is coming home to me,
now, as never before.

And his letters showed he still had a great capacity
to enjoy life. His buoyant spirit and astute observation
made his letters lively reading for his Letchworth
friends.

A Decision

But there was no great turning to Christ among the
Lisu. After five months in Tantsah he saw little result.
God's timing had not come. Perhaps, James thought,
he should write to Mr Hoste and offer for other work
temporarily, on the understanding that he would
return to the Lisu after a few months — maybe years.

It was the hardest decision he had ever made. As he
packed his bags and strapped on his sandals that last
morning in Tantsah he felt numb. But he had to make
a southward journey to the Tapu Pum mountains
before he need return to Tengyueh and write to Mr
Hoste. There was time to think on the mountain trail.

The trail wound down steep ravines walled by rock
faces, and then up stony paths and slippery ledges

before the villages could be reached.

Remote and poverty stricken, these Kachin hamlets were among the roughest of the mountains. Already weakened by the journey, James found the plain, red rice difficult to stomach. There was no meat or vegetable of any kind to help it down.

Fever

After a few days he fell back on his old plan of semi-starvation to let his digestion rest. But he soon found he was too weak to sing or to preach. Finally a fever set in and James headed in slow stages for Tengyueh.

The Emberys were startled to see the emaciated figure walk in. Pale and unshaven, he sat shivering with fever in the basket chair of their front room.

Tropical illness could be swift and fatal, the Emberys knew. No time was lost in administering such medicines as they had, and no trouble spared in buying the right food from the markets. It seems to have been malarial fever, aggravated by malnutrition and general weakness.

But he was young and he was strong. It was not many days before he was playing the little organ in the Emberys' living room. He had not merely needed medicine, food and rest. He needed his friends to pray with; to share the heavy burden on his heart. Was he right to stay on now and wait for the longed-for turning to God among the Lisu?

A visit to the healthy infant church in Paoshan reinforced his faith. Here was a clear proof of God's working among the Chinese he had preached to six years before. The most heartening aspect of it was that it was in the hands of a young Chinese pastor: a man, James wrote, with the 'heart of a shepherd.'

Friendship with Moh

James made a detour on his way from Paoshan to
Tengyueh to visit Moh the pastrycook at Hsiangta. He
was a man he enjoyed genuine fellowship with.

> Moh is a remarkably earnest Christian (he wrote
> on that visit). It is a treat to stay with him and see the
> way he witnesses for Christ down in the shop. He is
> the kind of man who takes the aggressive in a bright,
> happy-go-lucky way, . . . arguing with such in-
> genuity.
>
> Just now I am writing at this table in a big,
> upstairs room littered with all sorts of things — for
> order and neatness are not among his virtues! There
> are three beds, just the usual planks laid across a
> couple of forms and covered with straw mattresses. On
> the floor are big earthenware jars as high as your
> waist, piles of firewood, bales of cotton brought from
> Burma, stores of fruit, and all kinds of odds and ends.
> Moh is watching me write and is asking all about you:
> 'Is your Mother a Christian too? What is her
> venerable age? And can she read, like Mrs Embery?
> etc., etc.'

Moh's own mother was an opium addict and
hostile to his faith, and this was a sore trial to him. She
often threatened to drown herself because of the
disgrace of her son's allegiance to Christ. Her suicide
would have meant a lifelong shame to the family.

So Moh begged James to stay for a week and
counsel him. They spent several afternoons walking
the hillsides and calling on God to give wisdom and
direction to them both, and in the evenings they
prayed and read together in the small room behind the
shop. During these days James became quite certain
that he should make one last survey of his barren
fields. He was willing now to offer for work elsewhere
for a couple of years if God's time had not come.

A Last Journey

Two Lisu from Tantsah were with him when he set his face towards the mountains again. He had an unaccountable peace of heart. He would do nothing to persuade; nothing to appeal. He believed the Lisu would one day turn to God in great numbers. But now he would have the patience of the farmer. After the toil of ploughing and sowing and watering, he must wait for the harvest.

On the second night of his journey westwards, James and his Lisu companions stayed at a village he had often visited before. From the slopes above it the towering peak of Tapu Pum thrust sharply into the sky.

The villagers crowded round as usual, laughing and singing, clapping time to the songs he had taught them before. As night wore on, they lit their way to their homes, and James's host cleared a space for him to sleep on the earthen floor.

He was up at dawn, looking out to the western ranges and ready for an early start. As he stood waiting for the breakfast rice to boil he heard feet running.

'We must stay here for a day', his Lisu companions hurried in to tell him. 'There is a family who want to become Christians.'

He put his bags down on the floor and followed. Patiently he explained to the family the immensity of the step they were taking, and waited to see what they would do. They had already had the message explained on his several visits. He felt he needed to do nothing now but wait for God to move.

The family was ready. They were up at once pulling down all evidences of spirit-worship and destroying the demon shelves. Then they asked James to pray with them; they wanted the true God to receive them. Could they really become His sons and daughters?

He stayed for a couple of days to teach and advise these infants in the faith. And while helping them he had other callers: there was another family wanting to follow Christ, and another from the surrounding area. Eventually no fewer than seven families were pulling down their demon altars and asking to join the people of God.

This was heartening. It required no effort from James; just a restful communion with God throughout the proceedings. He acted as midwife and nurse, but the babies were born without any labour on his part. He stood aside and saw the salvation of the Lord.

Melting Pot

The travellers soon had to move on towards the Burma border where the wild Kachin territory lay, and the huts were primitive and squalid. At Melting Pot Village James was welcomed with unusual warmth. He hardly had time to talk to the people at their little evening meeting before the people were asking if he could help them to turn to Jesus Christ. No fewer than ten families destroyed their demon shelves. Eventually even the village shrine was pulled down; the greater part of the village wanted to serve the Living God. During these days James sent a letter home.

> Please excuse pencil again . . . under the circumstances in which I am now living. The one and only form this Lisu family possesses is not quite six inches above the ground. They never go in for chairs — no such luxury! and this family has not a table either. They have nothing whatever raised above the ground level, unless it be the cooking 'range' and I sleep just two or three inches above the earth floor. All

around me, or around the log fire rather, are Lisu, Lisu, Lisu! The good woman of the house is sitting next to me, with such a quantity of beads and ornaments as would give you neckache to wear. A couple of girls near by are watching me write and half-a-dozen boys on mats round the fire are learning to read the Lisu catechism. They are all interested in my writing, but I tell them to get on with their books.

But I am not going into further detail about the 'comforts' of this Lisu home, high up amid mountains and forest, as the most important thing is that my good host and hostess 'turned Christian' this morning, removing all sorts of things used in their former demon worship — bits of stick, pieces of paper, and much other trumpery — burning the whole lot in their centre-room fire. They turned quite wholeheartedly. They told me that they had long prayed to the spirits to give them a child, but without result, and asked if they might now pray to the true God for a son. I remembered the experiences of Sarah, Rebekah, Hannah and Elisabeth, and recommended them to go ahead. But they insisted that I must pray for them too. My prayers, they were sure, would be more effectual than their own!

Two other families in the village 'turned' at the same time. Altogether on my trip so far (not quite a fortnight) fifteen families have burned up all their idolatry and turned to God from four different villages . . . I never, now, try to persuade the Lisu to become Christians . . . I find that they are quite unstable and unsatisfactory unless they 'turn' with all their heart. When they really do this, I go round to each home and gather the family for a good long talk, explaining the step they are taking. Then we all stand and I pray with them, after which they go round chopping and tearing down all sorts of things and piling them on the fire . . . They seem glad to make a clean sweep while they are about it. The boys rather enjoy seeing things smashed up (boy-nature, you know) and help to ferret out suspicious objects. When they have swept the place clean — soot, cobwebs and all — they take me to the next house where people intend to 'walk the way of God' as they put it.

Cypress Hill

After some days spent here, James and his companions plodded on in torrential rain to Cypress Hill. In his first week here fifteen families became Christians, destroying every trace of their former slavery to spirits. James noted that it was the eighth anniversary of his landing in China: a fitting celebration, surrounded as he was with fifty or more young converts with all the hunger of the newly-born, wanting to know more of the things of God.

Turtle Village

He then set out for Turtle Village. On their arrival they found 24 families wanting to become Christians; just ready and waiting. Thirteen of these turned in one day, and they seemed to have a real understanding of what regeneration meant. He stayed for a full two weeks here, teaching and advising the converts. He was loath to leave this large group, but an urgent call came from some villages further south.

Mottled Hill

When he crossed the swollen waters that run down to the Irrawaddy and reached the lush slopes of Mottled Hill, James found no less than 49 families wanting to turn to God. They were not simply following each other, he found; there was an earnest seeking after God, a fear of being left outside His family, and a hunger for peace of heart after years of turmoil over spirit-worship.

Nor was it without opposition.

In one village, a man came running to him in a panic of fear. His family and four neighbouring families had broken with spirit-worship and its

associated objects and turned to Jesus Christ. Now the
spirits had turned in strength through this man's son.

It was surprisingly similar in scene to the story of
Luke 9, James found, when he followed the father.
The boy was screaming and foaming, writhing in
contortions on the ground. Bystanders were trying to
hold him back from leaping into the fire and finding
his strength superhuman.

Possession by evil spirits was not new to James
now, as it had been a few years earlier. He looked at
the circle of alarmed faces. These people, barefoot and
ragged, could neither read nor write: they were babes
in Christ only a few hours old. But they believed.

James led them in prayer aloud that the Name of
Jesus might prevail. And loudly they prayed with
him.

It was a great bulwark to their faith to see the boy
delivered. It was a clear demonstration that what God
said was true. They needn't fear any evil: God would
fight for them.

The Net Breaking

James was a careful and exact mathematician and kept
very precise records. He now calculated that 129
families had turned to faith in Christ out of the
darkness of demonism. This number represented
about six hundred people. It was a. large flock,
scattered from Mottled Hill to Tantsah, some eighty
miles of steep mountain country. He was now faced
with a new and pressing problem: who was going to
shepherd all these people?

He prayed about this without anxiety. It was so
clearly God who had moved; God would continue
what He had begun. It had been the most wonderful
journey of his life, this last journey looking for any

signs of God's working before turning elsewhere. God's time had come. And as always, it had been 'exceeding abundant, above all he had asked or thought': and it was only a beginning, he knew.

But he had now been travelling for several months and had not been able to get much sleep nor any privacy all that time. He would clearly not be able to cope alone.

And then he met an angel on the road.

James had stopped for a night in a village miles off the beaten track. As the evening drew on he was chatting with some Lisu in a doorway when he saw some men passing on the road. He stood up and peered through the failing light. One of them was no less an angel than Ba Thaw.

If there was anyone in the wide world he would have chosen to meet at this time it was Ba Thaw. To meet him in so obscure a place among the mountains just couldn't have been accidental.

Ba Thaw was visiting the few Lisu Christians he already knew. He had just arrived, and his eyes widened to hear of all that had been happening. Ba Thaw of course knew each village and understood the people. He was the natural shepherd God had provided for this little church.

James wrote of him later:

> The people here so took to him and he to them that he remained more than four months among them . . . The result is that not only have the converts been greatly helped and strengthened but others have been won. So I have come back to find 51 families in this district, instead of 49, all standing firm as far as demon-worship is concerned, and 36 additional families of Lisu converts in places I have not previously visited.

This young Karen is quite an exceptional man. He dresses like the Lisu, lives among them as one of themselves, and wherever he goes he is greatly loved. He is a better speaker of Lisu than I am, and is more capable in the shepherding of young converts. He is thoroughly spiritual, and I have no better friend among the Christians, tribal or Chinese, than he.

Ba Thaw went with James to Tengyueh for Christmas, both for a rest and to plan the next stage of the campaign.

There was no letter to write to Mr Hoste. No need for a change of plan. Only much to write home to his prayer-companions about a prayer-answering God. More than ever the new converts would need to be guarded and garrisoned by prayer. In writing to them James was buoyant:

I have been trying the last few nights to make up arrears of sleep. While at Husa (Southern District) I think I did not get to bed before 2 a.m. for ten nights in succession . . . We are now enjoying our usual winter weather — clear skies, dry roads and brown, withering grass everywhere. This is the time for itinerating, so I am due for the road again, after a needed rest behind the firing line. I must re-visit all these new centres with as little delay as possible.

You may ask: what of Tantsah? James went up there soon after Christmas, leaving Ba Thaw to visit and encourage the southern field. Many families at Tantsah, and especially at Cold Horse Village — where the Sword-Ladder Festival was held — had turned at last to Christ during these months of harvest. The people of this area were particularly clear and decisive. A new openness to the message prevailed, and family after family asked 'to walk the Jesus way', severing all connections with the demon-priest.

Rivers of God

Five great rivers run down from the world's highest
tableland through and around the foothills of Tibet.
Their fast waters bring life to plains as far apart as
central China, Vietnam, Burma and India. A sudden
rise in force and power, a sudden rush of great water in
the parched lowlands means that snow is melting at
high altitudes. It may have been raining in the
mountains.

Certainly James had a quickened sense that people
were praying for him at home. Thousands of miles
away, they were directly engaged in the work of God
among the Lisu, and concerned too in keeping James
himself filled with the Spirit of power. He knew
conclusively now that the prayers of God's people had
brought the harvest. He knew, too, that his cry to God
for deliverance in his own life and for the salvation of
the Lisu had been heard in Heaven. It was not being
heard at last *now;* it had been heard *then.*

'From the first day that thou didst set thine heart to
understand and didst chasten thyself before God, thy
words were heard' (Dan. 10.12). The long dark
months of testing were not God's mistake: they were
God's perfect plan.

Shanghai

Threatened appendicitis kept James at Tengyueh
soon after his visit to Tantsah, so he could not travel to
all the new groups of believers as he had hoped. An
Indian doctor advised him to have an operation as
soon as possible.

Meanwhile, Mr Hoste had written advising some
days at the coast. James had been in South-West China
for nearly ten years and it was strongly felt that he
should visit Shanghai and report on the work.

It was the last thing he really wanted to do. His work among the tribes, he felt, needed him more now than it had ever done before. But he set out southwards for the coast, to take a ship to Shanghai. He had not travelled far from Tengyueh before he was seized with agonising pain. He had no companion with him, and after a night of anguish alone in a Chinese inn, he was hardly able to travel on. Eventually the pain eased a little, and he was able to reach the boat for Shanghai. An operation was clearly needed now.

It was performed in Shanghai, and James's convalescent days were spent at the Mission's headquarters. Here was all the interest of a busy transit station: people coming and going from all parts of the interior. But James's heart was preoccupied with the pressing needs of his little flock in the Yunnan mountains. He steadied his faith on the promises of God.

> If I were to think after the manner of men (he wrote to his Prayer Circle) I should be anxious about my Lisu converts — afraid of their falling back into demon worship. But God is enabling me to cast all my care upon Him. I am not anxious, not nervous. If I hugged my care to myself instead of casting it upon Him, I should never have persevered with the work so long — perhaps never even have started it. But if it has been begun in Him, it must be continued in Him. Let us all who have these Tengyueh Lisu on our hearts commit them quietly into His hands by faith. 'He will perfect that which concerneth' us — and these Lisu converts too. And then let us give thanks for His grace to us and to them.

6   GOD'S DEEPER LESSONS

Shanghai
After years in remote parts of China, Europeans were often surprised how much they suffered from culture-starvation. While James was in Shanghai he was one of many prevailed upon to take part in musical evenings. He gave several piano recitals while he was convalescing, and his mini-concerts drew hungry listeners to CIM headquarters. In his orderly, methodical way he planned out each evening's performance and kept a handwritten programme with the date recorded to avoid repetition. One such programme reads:

Recital in CIM Hall. March 28. 1½ hours
Moskowski (Valse B)
Novelette in F
'Moonlight'
Chopin: 4 Waltzes and Prelude
Fairy Trumpets
Weber's Caprice in E
Rustle of Spring
Le Desir
Von Dittersdorf
Rachmaninoff

Before beginning to play James took the entire front off the upper part of the piano, insisting that the subtlety and accuracy of the sound were improved thereby. In any case, these were long remembered concerts. Many Europeans — missionaries and business-people — later would say, 'You ask me if I remember James Fraser? Well, I was there when he gave recitals in Shanghai.'

It had become James's habit, whenever he visited a Chinese city big enough to boast a shop with musical instruments, to 'rent' a piano for an afternoon and spend four or five hours living over the masterpieces again. This did not in any sense keep him in practice, but it was a needed outlet for the music pent up inside him.

During these days James developed a lasting and valuable friendship with D.E. Hoste, the General Director. Hoste seemed to many a rather remote and austere figure. His very appearance bespoke the military: so tall, erect and immaculate. One spoke to him with respect, if not awe.

James was his opposite in many ways but found they had much in common as well. Mr Hoste had become interested in the young tribal worker when he had first received letters from him. Now that he met him he found him to be a man of unusual spiritual power and understanding.

Hoste's task of supervising the work of nearly a thousand missionaries in the turbulence of early twentieth-century China was complex and arduous. James was impressed by the length of time D.E. Hoste allotted to prayer. Hoste was quick to point out that his time and energy was always saved by prayer and wasted without it; it was the lifeblood of the whole work of God in China. James was much influenced by the older man and joined him every day to pray — often for hours — for all aspects of the work. (On more than one occasion as they prayed James would find

Hoste pouring a cup of tea for himself at the far end of
the room while praying aloud.)

Return to the Tribes

But James was counting the days until he could be
back in the mountains and see how the infant believers
were getting on. A young American from Boston was
to go with him. His name was Flagg: he was twenty-
seven, and a graduate from Harvard and the Moody
Bible Institute.

They set out for Yunnan together: a long journey by
sea and then by land on horseback. Flagg found it
exhausting, unused as he was to riding day after day in
the mountains. He was taken first to see the eastern
tribal churches and then westward to James's home
territory.

> Up hill and down dale (James wrote), you never
> tire of it in beautiful Yunnan . . . I do all my travelling
> now on horseback . . . and have become so used to it
> that I do not care where I ride, so long as the horse will
> take it. In many places the road is literally as steep as
> your staircase and very broken too. Flagg declares that
> I would ride down the steps of the Washington
> Monument in Boston! Only to-day, my pony actually
> turned a somersault. It was in a place where the 'road'
> runs between banks only a foot or so apart, and he had
> hardly room to walk. With unusual thoughtfulness he
> gave me notice by falling right forward with his head
> on the ground. I got off over his head, and he plunged
> and kicked around until, somehow, he was lying on
> his back with his head where his tail had been!
> His neck was twisted in such a strange way that I
> wondered whether he was going to get up again at all.
> But he did, after more kicking and struggling, and
> began to eat grass as if nothing had happened. (Have
> you noticed how nonchalant horses can be?) Neither
> he, nor I, nor the Chinese saddle were any the worse;
> so I put on my right sandal which had dropped off,

got on the animal, and went on reading my Chinese
newspaper as before.

Wherever he travelled, Flagg noticed, James was at
his work of preaching. Sometimes they fell in with
other travellers and began conversation. Sometimes
they would join the company at a meal in a Chinese
inn. Sometimes they would call out their message in a
city street. Always there was an opportunity because
James was determined to find one.

James commented in a letter home at this time that
he felt a new power in his preaching these days and
greater strength in his life.

> If I am sure of anything, it is that your prayers have
> made a very real difference to my life and service. In
> preaching in the various centres visited, I have
> experienced power and blessing not known in former
> years. My chief request is always for prayer for the
> Lisu, but much blessing and help have come to my
> own life as well.
>
> So far as I know (he continued in the same letter)
> my Lisu work was undertaken at His bidding, which
> gives me confidence in asking your continued prayers.
> All our work needs to be, (1) In accordance with
> scriptural principles: (2) In agreement with the in-
> ward witness of the Spirit: (3) In harmony with the
> provisional working of God in our circumstances.
> Thus we shall have assurance within ourselves of His
> guidance, and shall find doors opening before us
> without our having to force them. Inward and out-
> ward guidance will correspond as lock and key, and
> we shall be saved from rendering service which, to
> Him as for us, is second best.

When he reached West Yunnan again he found the
young converts had grown both in understanding and
in numbers under Ba Thaw's shepherding. James left
Flagg at Tengyueh and followed the river towards

Bhamo, visiting Lisu and Kachin villages across the border, and he was encouraged on every hand to see the developments.

Mottled Hill Chapel

There was excitement and activity at Mottled Hill. High walls of bamboo matting were being erected and sturdy thatch made ready for the roof. The floor was being trodden hard and carpeted with rushes. Pine chip lamps were already provided, laid out on a large, flat stone.

It was the first chapel to be built in the western mountains.

James stayed at Mottled Hill for some weeks, but the building of a church was under way long before his visit. The land, labour and materials had all been freely given, and James noticed that the church was to outshine any other building in the village in size and architecture, simple though it was.

The opening ceremony, according to James, was a 'full-dress occasion.' Only a hundred could sit on the floor inside, so several hundreds, many from neighbouring hamlets, stood around outside and peered through the cracks in the walls and the doorway.

Worship tended to be an informal sort of affair, to put it mildly. As yet the Lisu Christians knew very little. The prayer most often used — in unison — at this stage was: 'God our Father, Creator of heaven and earth, Creator of mankind, we are your children. We are followers of Jesus. Watch over us today. Don't let evil spirits trouble us. We are trusting in Jesus. Amen.'

It was virtually impossible to keep a congregation quiet for long. But they loved singing and were innately musical, so James took pains to convey doctrine by the singing lesson.

'If you were listening outside,' he wrote, 'you might think some kind of comic drama was going on. It does not take much to amuse the Lisu!'

Whisky and Opium

Not surprisingly James was soon faced with problems of Christian ethics among the young churches.

Converts at Mottled Hill told him with glee about their prosperous opium trade. The Chinese government had sent out troops to destroy opium crops in the area.

'We had a prayer-meeting,' they told James, 'and asked God to protect our opium. We got knives and poisoned arrows ready to fight the soldiers if they came. But they didn't turn up, and we've made more money than ever on our opium this year, praise God!'

> They know my position (he wrote to his Prayer Circle), and I am telling them plainly that I cannot baptize anyone directly connected with the growth, use or sale of opium. Still, we must, I think, have broad enough sympathies to recognize genuine faith, even when it is accompanied by an almost untutored conscience. We must remember how, among ourselves, John Newton never had a conscience against the slave traffic[1] but 'enjoyed sweet communion with God', as he tells us, even when on his slave-raiding expeditions.
>
> There is such a thing as exercising faith for others (he had written from Shanghai a few months previously). When others are weak and we cannot be with them in person, God may be calling us to stand with and for them in spirit. He is able to quicken into life the very feeblest spark of desire for Him, or to use for their blessing the smallest amount of truth they may have apprehended. Indeed I have seen this before now,

[1] Rev. John Newton (1726-1807), author of many well-known hymns, including 'How sweet the Name of Jesus sounds'.

among the Lisu. They may know, often, what we call next to nothing; yet, if in any measure the grace of God is in them, they remember the little they do know, and it seems to sustain them. . . Let us all be imbued with the spirit of the Apostle who, though he had never seen the Roman converts, truly longed after them, that he might 'impart unto them some spiritual gift', and so far from absolving himself from responsibility, felt himself to be a debtor, 'both to Greeks and barbarians, both to the wise and to the foolish'.

Another question was about the rice-whisky. This was drunk copiously at weddings and similar festivities, and the results were invariably drunkenness and debauchery. Whisky was a real fire-water to the Lisu. The Chinese always said that 'for a Lisu to see whisky is like a leech scenting blood.'

The new converts readily admitted that they would be better off without the whisky in the normal way, but they wavered when it came to weddings. The break with treasured traditions seemed hard, though they admitted that the results of the alcohol were always disastrous. Several times James persuaded them to pour the stuff out for the pigs, who were cavorting about, hopelessly drunk, in no time. He wrote:

> The younger people of both sexes will as a rule heartily support me in my temperance crusade. They are the Radicals; the old people the Conservatives! In this case I got them to mix a lot of pig's food with the contents of the jar, to make it undrinkable.
>
> At another village they told me of a jar of whisky kept by a family which was just preparing for a betrothal feast. They badly wanted me to stay for the occasion, but I threatened to go away at once unless they consented to destroy the stuff. Finally the owner agreed and gave me the pig's food to mix with it.

Their 'Whisky' is not liquid, you know; it is just a mass of fermenting rice — the liquid is drawn off through a tube. I do not now destroy it all, as it is a pity to waste what is really a good fattening food for pigs, and I do not tip it out on the ground either, as pigs are worse drunkards even than the Lisu, and will drink themselves to death if you let them. One mixes bran, etc., with it — then they can feed it to the pigs at leisure, but would not touch it themselves. A novel form of temperance crusade, is it not!

Full House

The first Christian festival for tribespeople was held in 1917 at Tengyueh. They came by the dozen, crowding into the little mission house, where James and Flagg bravely catered for fifty residents as well as day visitors. Few of the mountain people had seen a city the size of Tengyueh before.

You would have been interested to see them when they first arrived (James wrote to his circle). Very few had even been in the city before. When they came to our house (we let them roam all over it) the girls, going round in a bunch from room to room, kept up a continual involuntary murmur of admiration and delight. It was like heaven to them! The men took things more calmly. Men with their big swords, gay satchels, chimney-like stockings and bare feet; girls with coloured turbans, tassels, beads, necklaces, rings, bangles and other ornaments — I wish you could have seen them! . . .

Every day, after Morning Prayers, I had them all in our chapel, teaching them to read the script . . . In the evenings I took them in singing. Besides 'Jesus loves me' and 'I've wandered far from God', which they knew already, I taught them 'God be with you till we meet again' and one or two other hymns. They sang so well that Chinese from the street would come in and sit and listen.

One day our new Consul came round to call on us

with the retiring Consul, Mr Eastes. The Lisu all
came crowding round them in the sitting-room and
outside, making all sorts of remarks and even feeling
their clothing! We explained to the Consul that they
must not mind, as our guests had little idea of the
proprieties.

'I should say not,' replied Eastes, taking it all in
good part, 'there is a fellow behind me stroking my
back right now!'

Afternoon sports provided more novelties for the
Lisu, the chief hilarity being the sight of James and
Flagg attempting the high jump and flat races. This
they would never forget.

More than eighty tribespeople sat down to the final
feast on Christmas Day, a culinary feat in this bachelor
household, but at least repaying the Lisu some of the
hospitality so freely given him in the mountains.
There was a special sense of unity in the family of God
in this festival. It was the first of many that took place
in the following years, a custom continuing where
Christian tribespeople are found to this day.

Patience

As he travelled from village to village among the new
groups of believers during the next few months, James
was awakened to the size of his job. Not only were the
young Christians scattered among the upland slopes
and remote fastnesses, but their understanding of the
faith was minimal. Some of them felt, he discovered,
that if they were now free from evil spirits and at peace
with God through Christ this was enough, surely.
Why have meetings? Why have a day of rest and
worship? They couldn't read, so why be governed by a
book?

James wrote to his colleagues at home and asked
that God would give the Lisu a 'spirit of wisdom and

revelation in the knowledge of Him' (Ephes. 1.17).
The work had hardly begun!

I am not painting a dark picture; I only wish to tell
you the real position of things as candidly as possible.
In some ways they (the Lisu converts) are ahead of
ordinary church-goers at home. They are always
hospitable. They are genuinely pleased to see me
when I go to their villages. They are sincere, as far as
they go; we see very little among them of the ulterior
motives commonly credited to 'rice Christians'. They
will carry my loads for me from village to village
without pay . . . and give me hospitality. But with the
exception of a few, very few, bright, earnest young
people, there are not many who wish to make any
progress or are really alive spiritually. Most of them
cannot be tempted away from their warm fires in the
evenings (these villages in the mountains are very cold
in winter) to come together and learn a little more,
even though I am in a nearby house which also has a
fire!

I have often in time past given way to depression,
which always means spiritual paralysis, and even on
this last trip have been much downcast, I admit, over
the state of the people. When at a village near Mottled
Hill, a month or more ago, I was much troubled over
all this, but was brought back to peace of heart by
remembering that, though the work is bound to be
slow, it may be none the less sure for all that. My
mistake has too often been that of too much haste. But
it is not the people's way to hurry, nor is it God's way
either. Hurry means worry, and worry effectually
drives the peace of God from the heart.

Rome was not built in a day, nor will the work of
building up a strong, well-instructed body of Lisu
Christians in the Tengyueh district be the work of a
day either. Schools will have to be started when the
time is ripe. There will be need of much visitation,
much exhortation, much prayer. It will not be done
all at once. The remembrance of this has cast me back
upon God again. I have set my heart upon a work of
grace among the Tengyueh Lisu, but God has

brought me to the point of being willing for it to be in
His time as well as in His way. I am even willing (if it
should be His will) not to see the fullness of blessing
in my life-time.

Absolute honesty was essential in all his reports of
the work if he was to expect spiritual support from
friends at home. His records of defeats are clear and
precise. Some groups of believers reverted to spirit-
worship. Some accepted a rumour that James was a
British agent looking for conscripts.

At the same time he was exact in his accounts of the
areas of growth. It seemed that some localities were
receptive, responsive and retentive. It was good
ground here and brought in a golden harvest; young
believers seemed to mature and stabilise in these
places. They were quickly able to stand on their own.

For his own part James found the work called for a
new kind of tenacity. Though he said little about it,
the physical hardships were considerable. Most of his
travelling in the mountains had to be done on foot. He
tried to convey his reasons for this slow method of
travelling in his letters.

> I have been out just over a fortnight (he wrote on
> one of these journeys) and am in Water Bowl Village,
> where I have fifteen Christian families . . . I expect to
> be about two months yet on this itineration before
> returning . . . When once in Lisu country, one seldom
> needs to travel more than fifteen miles a day, as the
> villages are within a few miles of each other. The hills
> are big: a day's journey will sometimes consist of a
> descent of three thousand feet to a plain, and then a
> similar ascent up the other side. But the cross-country
> roads are like ladders sometimes, and you have to ford
> streams, or jump precariously from rock to rock, and
> venture over crazy bridges. Sometimes you cannot
> even see the road before you, but just take it on faith. I

have no use for a horse in this kind of country. The hills are such that no one with any moral sense would ride up, and no one with any common sense would ride down.

He became so used to crossing swollen rivers that when his coolies refused to cross he would take the baggage over on his head first, and wade back to help the coolies across afterwards.

But damp living and poor eating was not really of great significance to him. 'I don't seem to notice these things like other people' he once said. He always enjoyed mountain life and looked forward to the climbs.

He had plenty of time to think about the principles of God's working as he tramped the trails.

Preparation, delay and growth (he wrote) are characteristics of God's working both in history and in nature. Scripture and the facts of nature meet, when James, exhorting us to patience says: 'The husband-man waiteth for the precious fruit of the earth, being patient over it.' The same principle applies to our own spiritual lives, and to our labour in the Lord. A mature Christian is not the product of a day or a month or a year either. 'It takes time' said the late Dr Andrew Murray 'to grow into Christ.' We must strike our roots down deep in the soil of the Word and be strengthened by long, long experience. It is a slow process, and it is right that it should be so: God does not want us to be spiritual mushrooms. It is true that in the Lord's work there is a place for haste — the King's business requires it (there is a right and a wrong haste), and there is assuredly a place for diligence, for earnestness. James Gilmour said he 'did not think we could be too earnest in a matter for which Christ was so much in earnest that He laid down His life.' You know it was said of Alleine that he was 'insatiably greedy for souls'. While it is day we cannot but be up and doing to the limit of the strength which God supplies. But the element of corroding care will enter into Christian work if we let it, and it will not help, but hinder. We cannot fret souls into the Kingdom of Heaven; neither, when they are once converted, can we worry them into maturity; we cannot by taking thought, add a cubit to our own spiritual stature or to anyone else's either. The plants of our Heavenly Father's planting will grow better under His open sky than under the hothouses of our feverish effort: it is for us to water, and to water diligently, but we cannot give the increase however we try. An abnormally rapid growth is often unnatural and unhealthy: the quick growth spoken of in Matt. 13.5 is actually said to be a sign of its being ephemeral.

In the biography of our Lord nothing is more noticeable than the quiet, even poise of His life. Never 'flustered' whatever happened, never taken off His guard, however assailed by men or demons: in the midst of fickle people, hostile rulers, faithless disciples — always calm, always collected, Christ the hard Worker indeed — but doing no more, and no less, than God had appointed Him; and with no restlessness, no hurry, no worry. Was ever such a peaceful life lived — under conditions so perturbing?

But we also, as He, are working for eternity and in eternity (eternity has already commenced for us): we can afford then to work in the atmosphere of eternity. The rush and bustle of carnal activity breathes a spirit of restlessness: the Holy Spirit breathes a deep calm. This is the atmosphere in which we may expect a lasting work of God to grow. Let us take care first of all that it is a work of God — begun and continued in God — and then let us cast our anxieties, our fears and our impatience to the winds. Let us shake off 'dull sloth' on the one hand and feverishness on the other. A gourd may spring up in a night, but not an oak. The current may be flowing deep and strong in spite of ripples and counter-currents on the surface. And even when it receives a temporary set-back from the incoming tide of evil, we may yet learn to say — as

Jeremiah once said under the most distressing circumstances — 'It is good that a man should hope and quietly wait for the salvation of the LORD.'

Reading Lessons

With the pastoral care of at least two hundred families James knew the time had come to produce a Lisu script and translate the first gospel and catechism.

When the farming season was at its height and chances for teaching therefore reduced, he went over to Myitkyina in Burma, to work on the project with Ba Thaw. The American missionaries in the city helped them to perfect a script for the language and James worked through the intense heat of the summer to finish Mark's gospel, a Catechism and a primer in Lisu. The manuscripts were ready for printing in Rangoon when James set out for the mountains again.

The Lisu writing James and his friends had devised — which became known as the Fraser script — resembled the English alphabet in capitals, but letters were used reversed or upside-down to represent sounds unique to the language.

Teaching the people to read was a laborious affair before printed copies of the books were available. The handwritten copies of Lisu writing had to be shared with a few at a time.

One group, James found, had become very particular about their position at the table after their first few lessons from a Lisu instructor who had just mastered the rudiments himself. James found that crowding around the one copy some had learned to read upside down and some sideways on, so they had to make sure they saw the writing from the same angle each time!

Turtle Village
He was greatly heartened to see the growth of the
church in the western district. On his return from
Burma his first port of call was Turtle Village.

> When I left Turtle Village last (he wrote to his
> Prayer Circle) there were fourteen families of Chris-
> tians, now there are 21. When I left Water Bowl there
> were twelve families . . . now there are nineteen. When
> I left Redwood Spur there were nine — now there are
> twenty . . . And this in spite of the fact that they have
> practically had no help of any kind for months. I hear
> that Melting Pot and Cypress Hill are the same as
> when I left them. They tell me that in the former
> village they have built a chapel (I have not seen it)
> where they hold regular Sunday services.
>
> In Turtle Village one of the elders of the place, a
> good old man, was seriously ill for many weeks. But
> he and all of them held on in faith and prayer and he
> pulled through. These people are great believers in
> divine healing, and such an experience strengthens
> their faith considerably. Altogether I think they have
> increased in strength as well as in numbers since I was
> last here.

When James's horse fell ill during his Sunday here
the people called him out to pray for its healing. Their
sure faith in the *power* of God perhaps needed to be
tempered by an assurance of the *will* of God.

> I confess I hesitated at first, not being used to just
> that way of doing things. But the people seemed
> surprised.
> 'Aren't you going to pray for your horse?' they
> questioned.
> So I went with them. We stood around the animal
> as I placed it in God's hands for life or death. Next
> morning I was glad I had done so while it was still
> living.

Twenty-five people were baptised while he was at

this village. During these early years James felt it to be vital to give guidelines to new believers on their conduct as Christians. Some felt he was mistaken here, and that it tended to legalism. However, when the Lisu later suggested having a book of rules James would not be party to it.

His account of the baptismal promise illustrates his attitude:

> Each one promised solemnly, not only to trust in the Lord Jesus for his whole lifetime, but to abstain from any connection with heathen worship, from whisky-drinking, immorality, opium-smoking or cultivation, and to observe the Lord's Day. I enjoyed the occasion immensely (I always enjoy a baptismal service) as we went down to their village stream that summer morning, separated the men to one side and the women to the other, on the river bank, and commended them all to God in prayer, under His open sky. I then immersed them, one by one, in the the swiftly running water, just below a thick plank bridge. Will you pray that they may be kept to their promises?

Skirmish with Death

Although James identified himself with the people as far as was humanly possible, dressing, eating and living as one of them, he could still make mistakes, even underestimate the strength of their traditions.

Staying one night in a Lisu village, he woke early in the morning and went out to pray. He was sitting under a tree and resting against it when he heard angry shouts.

Villagers crowded around him pointing at the tree. It was the demon-tree. The spirits would be furious and send disaster on the village, they said. A sacrifice must be made to placate them.

James was seized and bound to the tree. His arms were pinioned and his feet tied so that he could not move. It seemed as if death was very near.

He waited in pain and fear while preparations were made for the ritual sacrifice. Through his mind surged the countless promises of God. A heart fixed . . . a mind stayed . . . a life hidden. Whether by life or by death, he remembered again, God may be glorified.

After some hours of waiting James heard a discussion taking place among the villagers: maybe they could get money from him.

Eventually they surrounded him and proceeded to bargain with him for his life. He must buy a cow, they insisted, and they would sacrifice it in his place. He agreed to this reluctantly. He was released; he handed over the money; the cow was bought and sacrificed.

James was not slow to learn from this painful lesson. Satan's territory cannot be trifled with; he was on enemy ground. He walked more humbly after this, yet in joy that God had watched over every moment of the drama and delivered him from the very jaws of death.

The School of God
There were several other important lessons James learned during these years. Now and then he had bouts of great loneliness, in spite of the crowded hovels where he spent months at a time. It was one thing to be lonely when the work prospered; another thing to be lonely in deep discouragement.

He had prayed with great energy and hope for thirteen families in a village near the Burma border. He had spent hours alone on the mountainside in prayer for this village. His expectation was high when he met with the heads of the families who came to discuss the message of Jesus with him.

It was a strategic village. James knew that the whole group of hamlets in the area would be opened up for the gospel if this leading village began by accepting the message.

His discouragement was bitter when they rejected it.

As was his habit, he set off to find an empty room where he could pray this thing through. And it was in a little room found in a neighbouring village that the Lord met with him. He was reading II Chronicles 20 when he came to the words of Jahaziel:

'The battle is not yours, but God's . . . Ye shall not need to fight in this battle: set yourselves, stand ye still, and see the salvation of the Lord with you . . . Fear not, nor be discouraged: tomorrow go out against them; for the Lord is with you.'

He was deeply stirred by this remarkable chapter and spent the next few hours in 'fighting prayer'. At about midnight he felt victory, as his journal recorded.

> Seem distinctly led (he wrote) to fight against 'principalities and powers' for Middle Village. Have faith for the conversion of that place, and pray as a kind of bugle-call for the hosts of heaven to come down and fight for me against the powers of darkness holding these two old men who are hindering their villages and perhaps three others from turning to Christ. Have a good time of fighting prayer, then sleep in much peace of mind.

Early next morning James retraced his steps to Middle Village. The people there seemed much more responsive. Eleven of the thirteen families wanted to become disciples of the Lord Jesus.

'Victory,' he recorded, 'just as expected — hardly striking a blow!'

On the next day twelve more families came to ask if they too could accept the message he had brought to them and become children of God. It seemed as if the tide had turned.

Much of the next night James spent on the mountainside praying for a nearby hamlet which seemed hostile to his message as yet. Surely, he believed, God intended a strong group of believers in this district with some from every hamlet. It was victory all along the line when one fought through prayer.

He went along to the village next morning, taking with him one of the new believers from near Middle Village.

The people were cold and hostile. They did not want him there and they did not believe his message. So strong was their reaction against him that his companion turned against him too, renouncing his so-called faith and denouncing James as an impostor.

Numb and broken, James quietly retreated to his little empty room. It seemed a total defeat and his spirits reached a new low. But here God showed His loving kindness. A great sense of peace came over James when he humbled himself in his prayers. He had begun to assume victory would be automatic; village after village would turn to Christ if he prayed the fighting prayer. He saw again that there was no room for cavalier faith in the work of God; it had the wrong kind of confidence.

> Find considerable peace (he wrote) in just leaving the whole matter of these villages in God's hands. But the rebuff of spirit has been very severe, and I shall walk more humbly before the Lord — yes, and before Satan too, — after this.

The Price of Strength

One night James wrote his journal by the light of a pine-chip lamp at Mottled Hill:

> Thinking much of Stuart Holden's saying: 'I do not believe that any man is made victor save by blood of his own,' — 'resisting unto blood striving against sin' (Heb. 12.4).
>
> So often, as today, I have been unwilling to shed my own blood, so to speak, and have trusted in Christ alone — arm-chair trust, which has failed.

He found it was easy to slide into spiritual lethargy. After a long climb to reach a mountain hamlet, and several hours of preaching and teaching when he got there, he would fall asleep in a crowded, lice-ridden hut and oversleep in the morning. Mist and rain on the mountain kept him always in a crowd so there was no time or place to read and pray. The drift into spiritual weakness came imperceptibly: a slow decline to inertia.

An entry in his journal illustrates this:

> The whole cause of my defeat these two days is weakness of spirit. Under these conditions, any text you take fails to work. The spirit must be continually maintained in strength by unceasing prayer, especially against the powers of darkness. All I have learned of other aspects of the victory-life is useless without this.

Hudson Taylor observed that there is no possiblity of power in a life which is easy-going and which shrinks from the Cross. This truth was coming home to James during these months. It would be costly to maintain a close walk with God, a deep and continual cost every day of his life.

It is one thing to bear the cross; it is another thing to die on it. James had reached a new dimension in his

understanding of the corn of wheat which must fall
into the ground and die if it was to bring forth fruit.

This led him on to an allied truth.

'Everyone,' says A W Tozer, 'is just as holy as he
wants to be'.

James's journal at this time shows a hunger for
holiness of life. He had to spend a few weeks in
Tengyueh during the summer of 1918, because of a
badly infected foot. Something of his spiritual travail
is shown in the following entries in his journal.

> August 23. Considerable spiritual recovery . . .
> Enabled, practically, to clasp the foot of the cross.
>
> August 26. Thirty-two years old today. Quite con-
> scious of Mother's prayers. I am sure she is praying for
> me. Splendid time of prayer alone in my room.
> Enabled to get to the Cross and remain there. Have
> peace and rest of spirit. Preaching on the street in the
> evening.
>
> August 27. The Cross is going to hurt — let it hurt!
> I am going to work hard and pray hard too, by God's
> grace.
>
> August 28. Reading through Thomas Cook's *New
> Testament Holiness*.
>
> September 1. Yesterday evening, prayer out in
> gully.

And a week later, when he was about to set out on
long itineration:

> September 9. Very definitely and decidedly take my
> stand on I John 1.7 — Jesus Christ my Cleanser from
> all sin. Full of peace and blessing all the rest of the
> day. In the evening a Hohch'en man (Lisu) signified
> his willingness to accept Christ and came round for
> talk and prayer.
>
> September 11. Am proving I John 1.7 true, these
> days. Faith becames as natural as breathing. During
> the first few years I put forth too much self-effort with

James 4.7 which, perhaps, has no connection with inbred sin, but with the fight (offensive) against Satan's Kingdom in the world. In any case Thomas Cook's book has been a great help to me.

September 12. My weapon these days against sin and Satan — or rather, sin alone — is the love of God. How can we do despite unto the spirit of grace. 'The love of Christ constraineth us.'

September 16. Extracts from Jowett's *Passion for Souls:* 'The Gospel of a broken heart begins the ministry of bleeding hearts.'

'As soon as we cease to bleed we cease to bless.'

'We must bleed, if we would be ministers of the Saving Blood.'

'St. Catherine's prayers were red with sacrifice, and she felt the touch of the Pierced Hands.'

September 20. We should take up the whole armour of God before the 'evil day' comes, so that when it does come we may be able to stand. We need to strengthen the defences during every lull in the battle.

Setback

Over and over again James was to realise the uselessness of human effort on its own. He could work himself into the ground and have no effect on the people.

He wrote to his friends in Letchworth along this line after a major setback at Mottled Hill. Some of the believers had renounced their faith and gone back to spirit-worship.

The little church at Mottled Hill had been led by an intelligent and spiritual young man. James had high hopes he would become another Ba Thaw. However, while James was in Burma translating the first Lisu gospel a serious flu epidemic hit the Mottled Hill area and the young man died. This shook the faith of the believers profoundly.

The demon-priest was quick to seize his advantage.

> He gave out (James wrote) that he had seen the
> soul of this young man all by itself — i.e. neither in
> heaven nor in the place of their departed ancestors —
> holding a hymn book that I had given him and
> weeping. Hence Christians do not go to heaven, but it
> is all a hoax — QED.
>
> The orphaned child of this same man was taken ill
> not long after the father's death and they said that the
> spirit of the father had come back to 'bite' (attack) his
> own child. Do not imagine that the converts hear
> these things with a superior smile as we might. No,
> they take them very seriously.
>
> Many of the converts turned back (he added in
> another letter), and even those who did not, have more
> uneasy misgivings on the subject than they acknow-
> ledge, to me at any rate.

It was all very understandable, humanly. Nor was
Mottled Hill the only place where setbacks had
occurred. The truth he had emphasised in earlier
years — that regeneration is the work of God alone —
was applied in principle to the new situation. No
challenge, rebuke, persuasion or comforting, on his
part alone made any difference to anyone, even if it
seemed to at first. Only God's direct working would
produce lasting fruit.

He wrote to his prayer-circle:

> Broadly speaking God seems to have restrained the
> hand of the Evil One; and my colleague, Mr Flagg,
> thinks it a miracle that after only two or three days'
> teaching in some cases, so many of the converts have
> stood firm, against all the temptations they have had
> to face.
>
> I cannot insist too strongly on my own helplessness
> among these people apart from the grace of God.
> Although I have been now ten years in China and

have had considerable experience with both Chinese and Lisu, I find myself able to do little or nothing apart from God's going before me and working among them. Without this I feel like a man who has his boat grounded in shallow water. Pull or push as he may, he will not be able to make his boat move more than a few inches. But let the tide come in and lift his boat off the bottom — then he will be able to move it as far as he pleases, quite easily and without friction. It is indeed necessary for me to go around among our Lisu, preaching, teaching, exhorting, rebuking, but the amount of progress made thereby depends almost entirely on the state of the Spiritual Tide in the village — a condition which you can control upon your knees as well as I. Sometimes I feel that a village is 'grounded' — I do not mean in the sense of 'rooted and grounded' but in the sense of a boat grounded at low water! In such a case one can no more get the people together — i.e. to hold together and strengthen each other — than one could roll dry sand into a ball. They will be cold and unresponsive, and weeks or even months of teaching will not do much for them. Their 'prayers' are not answered as when the power of the Holy Spirit is with them. I repeat: one feels powerless to help in such cases, except to do all that is possible and then commit them to God.

Or to change the figure, the preaching of the Word of God in these Lisu villages is rather like vaccination. You insert the serum and the people are duly inoculated. But the result is different with different people and villages. In some the 'vaccination' is successful: the people go ahead in numbers and grow in faith. In other cases the 'vaccination' does not take! And the people revert to heathenism or to indifference. Does this apply to us also, on our plane and in our sphere? Have not we been inoculated by God's all-sufficient grace through the risen Christ (Rom. 6. 1-14) against sin — that deadly small-pox of the soul? And what has been the result? Has it taken — in your life? in mine?

Towards Maturity

Great spiritual stamina had been needed when James spent those first apparently barren years in the mountains praying for a turning to God among the tribes. Years had gone by without visible result. Then, in the lovingkindness of God, family after family and village after village had begun to cry to Him for salvation.

A new kind of stickability was needed now.

'This is not the end,' said Churchill when the war tides turned. 'This is not even the beginning of the end. This is the end of the beginning.'

Paul longed to see the Ephesians, 'mature, attaining the whole measure of the fulness of Christ' (Ephes. 4.13). James wanted more than anything now to see the tribal churches become steady, wise and mature. Years of labour were ahead of him.

Although there had been setbacks there were also encouragements.

> I do not want you to think I am discouraged about my Lisu work — far from it! I want you to know the truth, that is all. Much of what I say would probably apply to many places in the mission-field from which come rosy and optimistic accounts of the work — quite rightly, for it has that side! So has mine! and I am full of hope and am really sanguine about it. I have quite a number of Lisu who are honest and faithful as far as they go, and some who are especially, warm-hearted and earnest. They are hospitable people, generous, and comparatively guileless. Moreover, it is only right that I should say that we missionaries make our mistakes at times. We are not always wise in what we say and do. Also I am quite aware that whatever difficulties we may meet on our Lisu work, there are difficulties in all Christian service. I rather suspect you have them also at home . . . It was Dr Dale, I think, who said that we may change

our difficulties in Christian work but we can never escape them. I, for one, thank God with all my heart that I am just where I am and in the work I am now in.

Some of the Lisu converts — chiefly the younger people — are just splendid. They are the 'heres and theres' — the ones and twos — who will always give us most joy in our work for the Lord anywhere. A boy of eighteen who was with me for over a month last winter was of this kind — always bright and helpful. He would pray aloud every evening before going to bed and was so fond of hymns that a missionary passing through our station at that time called him 'the singing boy'. He is a hard worker and a splendid reader and writer. Two other young men from his village accompanied me for a fortnight some time ago, carrying my loads and helping me in every way. When they went back home they refused to take a single farthing in return for their work. One man in my southern district stood firm in his village when all the rest turned back. I visited his village, in the first instance, only because of his pressing invitation. Everyone there would testify to his being a total abstainer and keeping his family also from drinking liquor. No better testimony could be given of him than that he brings up his family to be of the same spirit as he. He could have given his eldest daughter — a bright, warm-hearted girl — in marriage to a fairly well-to-do family, but rather than give her to heathen people he got a much poorer young man, but a Christian, for her. It is a joy to meet that family: they all have that charm which comes from whole-heartedness and absolute sincerity.

China's Moody

Ting Li Mei was known as China's Moody. He was a humble, lovable preacher through whom many Chinese had become disciples of Jesus Christ.

When Ting asked to see something of the new tribal churches in the west James was overjoyed. For

one thing, Ting would give valuable advice; for
another, James would have a travelling companion
for several months. More than this, Ting's preaching
was just what was needed.

Ting found the squalor of the tribal villages quite a
shock. James was amused to be reminded of it: he was
all too used to it. At Turtle Village Ting asked James
if the people would be offended if he mentioned
personal hygiene in his talk.

'Go ahead,' said James enthusiastically.

With great tact and courtesy Ting suggested that
now they had become Christians just a very occasional
wash might be in the public interest. Also that they
might do their spitting outside rather than inside the
chapel.

Absolute astonishment was written on the faces of
the congregation. Some of them had never washed in
their lives, and as for spitting — most of them spat
every few minutes. Cleanliness had not automatically
followed the beginning of Godliness.

Ting was excited by what he saw of the infant
churches in the mountains.

One night darkness overtook them as they rounded
a heavily forested hillside. They trudged along 'a dark
and ghostly pathway' as James called it, exhausted
from their travels.

Suddenly, out of the darkness came the sound of
singing. They stopped in their tracks to listen. Slowly
it dawned on them that somewhere in the forest Lisu
Christians were singing hymns.

They followed the sound and came upon a newly-
built chapel at Water Bowl that James had never seen.
The meeting was being held in total darkness because
the Christians could not afford oil for their tiny lamps.

Ting's affection for little groups like this one was immediate. And James found his companionship a feast after so much loneliness. Once or twice he took Ting to see a view he specially loved, such as one near Turtle Village.

> The frontier of Burma was only a few miles away (he wrote) and we could see right down to the Irrawaddy Valley and Myitkyina plain. Ting has never travelled far outside his own country. But he is one of those people I try to emulate who find something interesting, something to be pleased about, just everywhere. If it is not the scenery, it is the costume of the people; if not that, it is some new plant or tree or animal never seen before, or some interesting local custom or legend.
>
> Up on the top of this range, he hit on a very peculiar tree — the most peculiar he or I had ever seen. It actually had six different varieties of leaf! One, and perhaps two, were parasitic growths, but not the others as far as we could see. It was fine to see the almost childish delight with which he gathered a specimen of each kind of leaf, and put them with some berries he was already saving. So pleased was he with the new things and scenes, that he suggested that we might have prayer together and thank God for it all. So, there and then, we three had a little prayer-meeting, sitting on a big rock on that great, high, cold mountain overlooking Burma.

James was also impressed by Ting's helper, a man called Pih.

> Pih is simply splendid . . . not much of a preacher, but a quiet, unassuming man of moderate education, willing to do just anything. Always there, when there is any drudgery or hard work to be tackled, he seems to find a way out of every difficulty, making things easier for everybody. You don't notice him much, but, like the boy's definition of salt as 'the thing that makes the

porridge taste nasty when there isn't any', he is the kind of man who makes things difficult for you, when you haven't got him!

American Partner

It was when he had parted with Ting at Tali that James met a young American who was to become one of the best-loved men God ever sent to the tribes, Allyn Cooke. James took to him at once, and Allyn described his first impressions of James as they travelled together to Tengyueh:

Fraser seemed young and strong physically. He was very sociable, for an Englishman. He spoke Chinese fluently, just like the people, though when occasion required he would use scholarly language. In his travelling outfit — home-made and kept for the road — he was sometimes taken for a coolie or even 'a foreign beggar'! But he always had the dress of a teacher with him, and at his destination would soon appear, to the surprise of strangers, as 'a perfect gentleman'.

And what a fellow-traveller he was! Well do I remember his thoughtfulness and unselfish care of others. He was never in a hurry, and would stop and talk with people on the road, always ready to do a good turn. He was kind to the animals, the coolies, the inn-keepers. And he was so practical! The pack-saddle was too heavy; he designed another. The new chum was unused to riding on the top of the load; Fraser insisted on his using the only foreign saddle. It was always the same — he was used to local conditions, he would explain, and did not mind them.

When we reached Tengyueh, I came to know more of his spiritual life and was much impressed by his talks from the word. He took me to some of his prayer-resorts outside the city, and I found that he fasted often, in a quiet way, before preaching. The influence of his life only deepened as time went on. Indeed, everything that I have as a missionary, I owe to Fraser.

Fighting Kachin

When James and Allyn reached Tengyueh a call came from a group of Kachin near Burma. Tribal chiefs had begun persecuting the Christians and blood had been drawn on both sides. Would James come and arbitrate?

These Kachin had no actual connection with James, but with American missionaries in Burma. But they needed someone who could speak Chinese, and had come a long way to find him.

Finally a rather shaky truce was agreed upon and relative calm restored. But here was James's opportunity. The Kachin of his own district, west of Tengyueh, were entirely unreached with the message of Jesus Christ. James could not speak their language (Atsi Kachin) but these people could. As he had come so far to help them, would they be willing to send messengers to 'his' Kachin?

They promised to think it over.

Mountain Festival

Modern music festivals have none of the excitement and happiness of that first big rally in the mountains. It was the Christian festival of Turtle Village.

Hundreds of tribespeople flocked in from remote villages in the heights and valley hamlets of the Salween gorges. They brought their food with them and slept just anywhere. Their singing could be heard echoing over the canyon miles away, for the mountains were good conductors of sound.

In the middle of all the activity James had a particular encouragement. Twenty Kachin tribespeople from 'his' area had shyly come to join in the festivities. They were ragged, wild-haired and barefoot. They could neither read nor write. But dimly they understood that there was a welcome for them to join the people of God.

God had invited them to become His sons and daughters.

7 THE NET BREAKING

Lisu King

The firelight flickered over the brown features of the Lisu tribesmen from the Cold Country sitting in Moh's back room. Their dark eyes had shadows of doubt; their faces were hard.

Moh leaned forward. 'You say your legend tells that one day you will have a king. I tell you — He has come! His name is Jesus, *Yesu*. That's why you are called *Lisu*. You are the people of Yesu.'

The tribesmen shook their heads.

'What's the point of having a king nobody can see?' they asked with an edge of contempt. 'Our legends say he will be a man like ourselves and will bring us our own books.'

Silence fell as they stared at the flames.

Suddenly Moh had an inspiration. He turned to a pile of papers in the darkened corner by the doorway. Buried in the pile was a dusty photograph. He wiped it against the sleeve of his gown.

'Here is your king,' he announced decisively.

The tribesmen peered at the picture. There stood James and his friend Flagg, photographed in Lisu dress.

Now they were interested. The legend handed down from the mists of time had told of a king who would come to the Lisu: a tall, white man bringing them books.

Moh put his fingers on the photograph of James. He reinforced his somewhat dubious line of argument.

'Look, here's your king at last! He's white and he's making books.'

All in a good cause, he thought to himself. Now maybe they'll invite James to their area.

Sure enough, after a few weeks they were back at Moh's house. Their people in the Cold Country were interested in the story of the king. They would like to hear more.

Moh sent a runner with a postcard to James.

Cold Country Miracle

The postcard arrived while James was surrounded by the crowds at the festival. The Cold Country was four days' journey away and he had already promised to go back with the Atsi Kachin to teach them after the festival.

He recalled how the Cold Country people had refused to accept his message five years previously. And now they had sent to ask him to come! He was in a dilemma.

At last he turned to Allyn Cooke, who had left his study at Tengyueh to join the festival. Allyn had little knowledge of Chinese and no Lisu at all. Would he be willing to go? James asked.

With considerable courage Allyn agreed, and found himself pitched head first into tribal work.

He did not know the language; he hardly knew the people; and nobody, it appeared, knew the way.

Even Moh was unsure of the trail to the Cold Country, so when Allyn and his two Lisu companions arrived at Moh's house they had to wait till market day for their Cold Country guides. Sure enough, the

headman — Big Tiger — came down to the market
with several others, partly to buy whisky and partly to
escort the visitors. New Year celebrations were near
and so extra provisions were needed, but Allyn was
puzzled about the copious gallons of whisky they
bought.

The guests were warmly received in the four host
villages, and while preparations for the festivities were
under way Allyn was able to use his little Chinese to
explain his message. The invitation from the people
had signified a willingness to talk: nothing more.
Allyn had brought a few Chinese books with him just
in case the people wanted to turn to the Lord, though
books were not generally used until a stand for Christ
had been made.

The elders of Big Tiger's village held a discussion
soon after Allyn's arrival.

'We can't become Christians just now,' they came
and told him. 'It would be a waste of good whisky.
When we've finished the whisky we'll talk it over with
you again. Stay till it's all finished and see what our
people feel then.'

So the drinking began.

The drinking and dancing were soon followed by
scenes of appalling drunkenness and debauchery.
Every evil influence seemed to be let loose; the very
atmosphere was sinister. The people's faces in the
firelight were darkened and haunted; their every act
degrading and bestial.

Allyn felt emotion building up inside him as
he watched the proceedings. He and his two Lisu
companions sat alone, unable to convey to the people
that God is light and in Him is no darkness at all.

Finally the main feast day came. Allyn was given a
special chair in the headman's room.

One after another tribespeople staggered in, much
the worse for their drunkenness, to prostrate themselves before the spirits of their ancestors. They
knocked their heads several times on the earth floor
before the tablets, in worship of Satan. Allyn was
obliged to watch.

Suddenly a deep-seated emotion welled up inside
him. He fought to control it for a minute but at last
broke down in tears, shaking with sobs as he sat in the
chair.

Big Tiger was astonished.

'What's the matter? Is something wrong?' he asked
in Chinese.

'I am weeping because you are lost. You are on your
way to darkness for all eternity without Jesus Christ,
and I can't do anything to save you,' Allyn replied in
broken Chinese.

A powerful sense of the Presence of God came over
them. 'If you feel so bad about it,' said the headman,
trembling, 'we'll stop right now. We'll throw away the
whisky. Tell us about God and pray to Him to save us.

Allyn and his companions did their best to explain
to the headman and his family what it meant to
become a child of God. It was not easy to convey fully
the meaning of the Cross, of deliverance from sin and
of eternal life in the few words of Chinese they both
understood. But the Holy Spirit opened the mind of
this man and his family.

There and then Big Tiger and his family destroyed
all the objects of demon-worship from the house.

Then Big Tiger led the way to the Spirit Tree
(Allyn remembers). It was just an old stump, too big
to cut down. Incense and bowls for food stood on the
shelf attached to it. Big Tiger broke the bowls and
tore out the shelf, burning everything that could be

burned. A little hut stood nearby with incense for spirit-worship. They tore it down and carried it all to the bonfire.

Villagers who had watched and overheard came under the same conviction. All the whisky was poured out to the pigs. Voices kept calling to Allyn from house after house to come and help pull down spirit-shelves and tell the people how to be saved.

> Before nightfall (Allyn writes) the whole village had professed to believe. Within a few days the people of Rock Cave River, the next hamlet, had followed suit, and then of Big Nitre River, though these were slower in making the break.
>
> When I had to return to Tengyueh to continue my language study my two Lisu companions remained to instruct the people and carry on the work.

Sequel

Some months later one of the Lisu companions turned up in Tengyueh with a large order for Lisu books. He explained that such a movement was taking place among the tribespeople in the Cold Country that the two Lisu teachers hadn't been able to cope with the enquirers. The movement had gained its own momentum. Young converts of a few days' experience were helping others. Wherever the two Lisu teachers had gone, it seemed, God had been there before. Some of the people were learning to read Lisu already and they had collected money to buy books and carry them the six-day journey over the mountains.

It was all so clearly a work of God and not of man. Allyn Cooke had seen the start of it, while James had never even been to many of these places.

So great was the need for books now that James and Allyn had to go down to Rangoon to hurry the printing, a sixteen-day journey over the high ranges of the border. It was a journey of breathtaking beauty, made even more enjoyable because of its mission.

They parted on the return journey: Allyn to continue his studies at Tengyueh and James to see the Cold Country villages for the first time.

> I wish you could have been with me (he wrote) as I went from village to village, to have seen the royal reception they gave me! And you would have shared in it too. What with the playing of their bagpipes, the firing off of guns, the lining-up of all the villagers, men and women, young and old, to shake hands with you (they use both hands, thinking it more respectful) you have a feeling of being overwhelmed — an 'overweight of joy'.

James stayed in the area for several weeks. And exhausting weeks they were. The people were insatiable in wanting to learn more: 'tumbling over themselves in their earnestness' as he put it. 'Almost the whole village would stay with one all day long, crowding the room to suffocation round the fire.'

It was the rainy season, so James was more or less permanently damp, trudging from village to village in the pouring rain. He ate whatever food they gave him, and slept on a bamboo mat on the crowded floors.

> If this is not an answer to prayer (he wrote) what is it? . . . Some things specially please me about this new Eastern district. In the first place, the work was practically begun and has been almost wholly carried on by the Lisu themselves, however raw and poorly trained. They have not only passed on the little they know, but have taught others to teach in their turn. So many of these young people and children had learned to read and write, in an elementary way, that I was flooded with little notes and have not yet found time to read them all.

Another matter for thankfulness is that the proportion of Christians to heathen is so large. In some vicinities scarcely any heathen families remain. This is a great advantage, as it considerably lessens temptation and complications. Last but not least, practically all the converts agree not to plant opium. This will pave the way for baptisms and the formation of churches in due time . . . They want to have a large gathering at Christmas. Will you pray that it may be a time of much blessing — as also the Christmas we hope to celebrate again at Turtle Village.

Up to the present I find that in this new district alone there are over 240 families professing to be Christians. The total number of converts in the districts previously worked, of which I have sent you maps, is over 180 families of Lisu and more than twenty families of Kachin. So there are now, in all, about 450 families of tribespeople for whose teaching and shepherding we are responsible. This represents over two thousand young and old, for the average family out here numbers about five persons.

Eventually James was weakened by overstrain, went down with a fever and had to get back to Tengyueh.

The Letter-Writer

It was useful to be able to write graphic letters. A lady in Letchworth assured James she had come to know the Lisu so well through his letters that they could be living in the next street.

This was just what he wanted. He depended so much on his prayer supporters that he sent maps of the villages and detailed reports of the people. He wrote to each supporter separately, and answered all their questions.

When James had spent some weeks among the Atsi Kachin (where he found forty families wanting to become Christians before he even arrived) he found the bleak heights and the poor food more than he

could cope with. To give himself a break he went
down to a Chinese inn on the plain. It was better than
a Riviera hotel after the Kachin hovels.

For lodging only, including firewood and water
(also an inn coverlet — ahem — if you care to use it)
we pay twopence a day each . . . We borrow our pots
and pans from the landlord — this is thrown in with
the twopence. The Lisu I have with me go out each
morning to buy food . . . Sometimes I go myself — and
you might smile to see me with a basket of vegetables
on one hand and a string of cash in the other, or a bit
of fat pork dangling from a slip of bamboo, walking
along the roughly paved street of the market between
the thatched stalls of the vendors. But I take a positive
delight in doing just what the Chinese do. They boil
the rice first (I must learn how to do this, you know)
over a gipsy fire against the wall of the inn-passage.
When it (the rice) is done they put the lid on and kind
of roast it by the side of the fire while they boil the
vegetables. The latter they first chop up with their big
knives, then fry, then pour water on and boil. This
method of frying and boiling makes the stuff tasty as
well as cooked. There is an angry *fizh-zh-zh-zh-zh*
when they pour on the water, and sometimes a flash in
the pan.
When all the stuff is cooked they reach the bamboo
table down, put the basins, bowls, chopsticks and
ricepot on it. Perhaps the landlady complains that we
are making her table all black by putting the rice-pot
down on it: if so, we go and get a piece of rough
Chinese paper to put under it. I say grace in Lisu and
we set to. You needn't pity me living on 'Chinese
Food' such as you can get at a place like this: it is as
delicious as it is nourishing. Flagg, who has just
passed through here on his way to Tengyueh from
Bhamo, said I was looking well though I have been
living on native food for over three months. I am
likely to go on living on it for another month or more
yet too. During all this time I have not tasted foreign
food of any kind — no bread, butter, porridge, milk,

tea, coffee, cocoa, or sweet things, nor do I have any
particular desire for them. In Lisu and Kachin villages
I rather feel the lack of fruit, but down here you can
get pears of a sort, persimmons, bananas, pineapples,
etc., at present. I have tasted as good bananas here
(seven a penny) as I have ever had at home . . .

It is market-day today and the street is just beginning to hubbubify. You can see no less than seven
races each with its own distinct language — Chinese,
Shan, Palaung, Achang, Lisu, Jinghpaw, Kachin,
Atsi Kachin. I would make race No. 8 wouldn't I? You
can tell all of these races apart — except the two tribes
of Kachin — by the dress of the women, and the
women are most in evidence on these markets in this
part of the world. They bring in all sorts of produce
carried either in two baskets by a pole over the
shoulder, or else in one on their back, dump it down
by the side of the street, sit there and wait for
buyers . . . The shopkeepers put their stuff outside
the shops on stalls, displaying a hundred-and-one
different kinds of foreign and native articles — lamps,
lanterns, kerosene oil, mirrors, scent, woollen socks,
boots, shoes, quinine and patent medicines, soap,
pocket-knives, handkerchiefs, pencils, etc., etc., together with a lot of cheap jackery, frippery and
fruppery, janglery and banglery, around which you
commonly see the maidens and youthful matrons of
the various tribes — their hearts entirely set on it all,
and with a big-eyed 'wish-I-could-afford-to-buy-it'
look on their faces . . .

If you were to see the Kachin women and girls,
you might pronounce them the wildest specimens of
humanity you had yet met. You might even be as
afraid of them as they would be of you! The Kachin is
a straightforward, blunt kind of individual, without
any of the twists and turns of the Chinese. He does not
always appear to be saying, 'I wonder what that
foreigner has up his sleeve anyway.' The Kachin girl
is the most in evidence, for the men do not go to
market much, and the older women not so often as the
younger. You are free to chat with her anywhere and

everywhere: she looks at you straight in the face with
an expression of mingled indulgence, delight, and
amusement, as you try to stumble out your meaning
in broken Atsi. She is an impulsive, demonstrative
creature: you can just watch the progress of her
thoughts, for she does all her thinking on the outside
of her face.

Last market day I met some Lisu from the Upper
Salween on the street. They were carrying tremendously heavy loads of betel-nut to sell. 'Come up to
our village and teach us,' one of them said — his
village is about sixteen days' journey away. 'We will
give you food — rice and pork — as much as ever you
want.' Though he meant it sincerely, he was too busy
to do more than just invite me. That district must be
evangelized, but I want to find suitable nationals to go
first.

At the same time James was absorbed by the
practical implications of his prayer-supporters' part in
the work. He wrote the following important letter
home about it from his Chinese inn.

There are many things I wish to tell you about (he
wrote), I want to give you as good an idea of the
people, their habits, their dress, their food, their
language, their ideas, their peculiarities, as I possibly
can. I want to tell you all about my plans for the self-
support of the work — a subject on which I feel very
strongly indeed. But I want to distinguish between
temporal self-support and spiritual self-support. The
former is eminently desirable and practicable, the
latter is almost impossible for, perhaps, generations to
come.

They — the Lisu and Kachin converts — would be
easily able to support their own pastors, teachers and
evangelists by well-advised cultivation of their own
ample hillsides, and it is fitting that the mountains
should bring forth supplies for the needs of those
whose feet are beautiful upon them; but spiritually
they are babes, and as dependent upon us as a child

upon his mother. They are dependent on us out here for instruction, guidance, organizations; but they are dependent on the home churches in England and America in a deeper sense, for spiritual life and power. I really believe that if every particle of prayer put up by the home churches on behalf of the infant churches of the mission field were removed, the latter would be swamped by an incoming flood of the powers of darkness. This seems actually to have happened in church history — churches losing their power and life, becoming a mere empty name, or else flickering out altogether. Just as a plant may die for lack of watering, so may a genuine work of God die and rot for lack of prayer.

One might compare heathenism with a great mountain threatening to crush the infant church, or a great pool of stagnant water always threatening to quench the flames of Holy Ghost life and power in the native churches, and only kept dammed up by the power of God. God is able to do this and much more, but He will not do it, if all we out here and you at home sit in our easy chairs with our arms folded. Why prayer is so indispensable we cannot just say, but we had better recognise the fact even if we cannot explain it. Do you believe that the Church of God would be alive today but for the high-priestly intercession of the Lord Jesus Christ on the throne? I do not: I believe it would have been dead and buried long ago. Viewing the Bible as a record of God's work on this earth, I believe that it gives a clear, ringing message to His people — from Genesis to Revelation — YOU DO YOUR PART.

Have you ever thought it strange that God allowed nearly eighteen centuries to pass before opening the gospel door to more than half of the human race — India, China, and Japan? Though the church cannot shirk responsibility for the fact, I still believe God had a purpose in it. I believe that He tried the evangelizing of the heathen — if I may reverently say so — many times in former centuries. But His church did not rise to the occasion: she was too encumbered with error

and corruption, too powerless, to nourish the children
to which she gave birth; and such sporadic efforts as
were put forth by earnest men in past centuries to
form churches in (what we now call) the mission-field
never resulted in anything live and permanent. At the
time of the Reformation, she, the Church was only
just beginning to come to her own, and it was not
until after the Evangelical Revival of the eighteenth
century that God, as it would seem, deemed her fit and
strong enough to bear and nourish children in the
midst of the great heathen systems of the world. It is
rather striking, to me, that Carey's departure for India,
which we regard as the birth of the modern missionary
movement, took place just two years after the death of
John Wesley, the central figure of the great
Evangelical Revival.

And now, the mother-church of Protestant
countries is well able to nourish the infant churches of
the Orient, not only in regard to men and money but
also in regard to a steady and powerful volume of
intercessory prayer. Applying this to the work among
the Tengyueh tribespeople, I feel I can say that you,
and those God will yet call to join you in this work,
are well able to sustain the spiritual life of the Lisu
and Kachin converts, as well as to increase their
number many-fold. And just as I feel that God
has waited until the home church attained strength
enough to nourish her children — before giving her
her present large and growing family in the mission-
field — so, it may be, He has been preparing you for
the unseen and spiritual parenthood of these infant
Lisu converts here, however many thousand miles
separate you from them.

You may perhaps say: 'Do you get the converts
themselves to pray as they ought to?' This is a very
natural question and I can best answer it by saying
yes — and no. I get them (or try to get them) into the
habit of prayer, but it is only the cry of the babe they
utter, not the strong pleading of the adult. They only
know how to pray with anything approaching in-
tensity when their friends are sick and their prayers in

such cases seem to be remarkably effectual, but they know nothing of pleading for the salvation of souls. Unfortunately it is not many, as yet, who see that it matters much whether others are saved or unsaved. Their prayers are almost entirely selfish, just as a baby's cries are. One does not think hardly of a baby for that reason! Moreover I can go farther and say that large numbers of converts do not realise what salvation means, even for themselves. More will do so later on, given time, instruction, and something in the nature of a revival; but at present their knowledge is very elementary and their attainment small. They have not yet grown to military age in this spiritual warfare; they are babes in God's nursery, not warriors in God's army. But you have centuries of Christianity behind you, you have had Christian education, Christian influence, an open Bible, devotional helps, and many other things to help you in your growth to spiritual maturity. So now you belong to those of full stature in Christ, who are able to 'help . . . with power against the enemy'. The vast difference between you and them is that you are 'grown up' in Christ, while they are babes and sucklings; and the work of pulling down Satan's strongholds requires strong men, not infants.

They — the Lisu and Kachin converts — have their difficulties, of course, and sometimes persecutions, but in speaking of their present inability to fight in this spiritual warfare, I mean warfare in a purely spiritual sense. I will not labour the point: you will see from what I am saying that I am not asking you just to give 'help' in prayer as a sort of side-line, but I am trying to roll the main responsibility of this prayer-warfare on you. I want you to take the BURDEN of these people upon your shoulders, I want you to wrestle with God for them. I do not want so much to be a regimental commander in this matter as an intelligence officer. I shall feel more and more that a big responsibility rests upon me to keep you well informed. The Lord Jesus looks down from heaven and sees these poor, degraded, neglected tribespeople. 'The travail of His soul' was for them too. He has waited long. Will you not do your part to bring in the day when He shall 'be satisfied'?

Anything must be done rather than let this prayer-service be dropped or even allowed to stagnate. We often speak of intercessory work as being of vital importance. I want to prove that I believe this is actual fact by giving my first and best energies to it, as God may lead. I feel like a business man who perceives that a certain line of goods pays better than any other in his store, and who purposes making it his chief investment; who, in fact, sees an inexhaustible supply and an almost unlimited demand for a profitable article and intends to go in for it more than anything else. The DEMAND is the lost state of these tens of thousands of Lisu and Kachin — their ignorance, their superstitions, their sinfulness; their bodies, their minds, their souls; the SUPPLY is the grace of God to meet his need — to be brought down to them by the persevering prayers of a considerable company of God's people. All I want to do is, as a kind of middleman, to bring the supply and the demand together.

A Lisu Wife

Many of James's friends among the tribespeople thought it was high time he got married.

'We'll get you the best girl we can find in the mountains,' they offered enthusiastically. Many suggestions were made to him by Christian fathers whose daughters were of marriageable age. One very persistent Kachin headman actually went as far as trying to arrange a wedding between James and his daughter. The only way James could extricate himself was by packing his bags and leaving the village.

Most of the mountain people had never seen a white woman. James heard one tribeswoman recount her sight of one in the marketplace: her strange clothes, her slim waist and the courtesy shown her by the white men. It was all very extraordinary. As James would not oblige them by bringing one with him they decided white women were obviously in short supply. But they sensed his loneliness and noticed his affectionate nature and love for children. What they were not able to know at the time was the cost it had been for James to *give* himself to them for the sake of the gospel. He had freedom as a bachelor, but might have said like the centurion to Paul, 'At a great cost obtained I this freedom.'

Mission-House Made Mission-Home

Mrs Flagg was a good cook. She had imagination. The bachelor house at Tengyueh was transformed when she arrived. Flagg had waited patiently for her during her six years at the coast. She was a superb accountant and HQ had thought her indispensable there, but when she reached Tengyueh and married Flagg she also showed herself quick to learn the language and efficient at managing a household.

'She makes the best bread I have tasted in China,' James wrote home.

Mrs Flagg had an understanding heart and felt James and Allyn ought to stay more in the mission-home and do less roughing it in the mountains. '*Now* she is your friend for ever, isn't she?' he wrote to his mother. Mrs Flagg also noticed when encouragement was needed: it was good for James and Allyn to have someone to report back to, as James had to the Emberys in earlier days.

Mountain Hut

But James wanted to get on with translating John's gospel and teaching the Lisu and so he set off for the mountains.

His new home consisted of a bamboo shed six thousand feet up, at Turtle Village. The village itself was almost entirely Christian.

The walls of his shack were of bamboo matting and the roof of rough thatch. The earth floor was hollowed out in the centre for a log fireplace. He had a Lisu-made bamboo bedstead, table and stool. A coffin-plank he borrowed made a solitary shelf on which he put his books and papers, medicines, tins of cocoa and condensed milk and a tin of biscuits sent by Ba Thaw's wife. (Ba Thaw came and shared the shed with him for some weeks to help with translation work.)

The people of the village made themselves at home in his house. They investigated all his things and sat around to watch him write. Children in particular would sit around and chat to him. Little Miss Kung was a special friend. She was ten years old.

> She has big brown eyes, round and full like a deer's, a bright face and an eager, childish smile . . . I wish you could hear her prattle: you would realize two things — first that these children are not lacking in quick intelligence, and secondly that they are just flesh and blood children like ours in England. How she will chatter! These children live such natural lives; they know all their hills and valleys by heart, know the names and habits of all the animals, birds and insects to be found there, as well as all about the trees, shrubs, etc., found on their hills. They will sit and make necklaces of red berries, or plait bracelets out of wild grass while they tend cattle. And she will talk about these and many other things. She will tell you all the affairs of the village — how So-and-So lost something, and then his mother scolded him, at which he got sulky and ran up and slept in the hut on their buckwheat field, then how his sister saw him and told his uncle, what the latter said and then what someone else said, and how they had a quarrel about it, etc., etc., all of

which details do not interest me half as much as the charming vivacity of the child who is telling them.

He loved teaching the children to sing. The tribespeople were musical enough to sing in parts easily, and James taught them to read simple music by a method he made up himself. Hymns were a way to convey doctrine. One of the hymns they learned told the outline story of the Old Testament in numerous verses, and another did the same with the New. As there was no Lisu Bible yet, this provided at least an introduction.

Self Support
The mountain people were poor, very poor. James knew how poor because he shared their poverty. To them all Europeans seemed well-off. Curtains, for example, seemed a wanton waste of cloth to the Lisu. (Anyway, why did the foreigners have such an obsession about privacy? What were they trying to hide?)

Lisu food was subsistence level only, and their resistance to illness was very low. When an epidemic struck there would be death on a large scale. Their homes, too, scarcely kept out the bitter winds of winter in the heights.

But the more he thought about it, the more certain he became that the tribal churches would only grow strong if they were financially independent from the start. To be self-propagating they would have to be self-supporting.

It would have been much easier to give them money. Plenty of people in England and America would have sent money to build churches and pay pastors. But James saw (and he was not alone in this) that foreign money and foreign control would build a foreign church, and a weak one. The Lisu had to learn straight away that they must give to the Lord out of the depths of their poverty. Their own sacrifice would support their own chapels and evangelists.

James encouraged voluntary and unpaid preachers to go out on evangelism around the vast unreached areas of the border mountains. They were to go where the Spirit of God guided them and trust Him to provide for them. If they left families behind the local Christians were to provide for them while the trip lasted.

He did not pay his helpers either. When volunteers offered to carry his things or bring books to the village James did not pay them. No one was to gain money by serving the Lord.

Out of their poverty James let the people buy their own gospels, hymnbooks, notebooks and pencils. If they had no money at all they had to save up.

When the people wanted to build a meeting-place he left them to it. The buildings themselves were not regarded as of prime importance anyway; but they kept the rain off their heads. All the materials and labour were their own, right down to the oil in the lamps. If they couldn't afford oil and were out of pine chips they prayed and sang in the dark. James paid for nothing.

Although indigenous principles are widely accepted in the work of missions today, the idea was relatively new in the 1920s. Not that James was its pioneer by any means. It was in discussion with other workers that the idea came to him to start with.

We do not consider ourselves rich as compared with other Europeans out here, but we are rolling in wealth compared with these poor tribespeople, and are tempted to feel mean, burdening them in any way. But I am convinced that we ought to do it. So I let them carry my baggage on their backs from village to village, sometimes as far as twenty miles, and never offer payment. They do not expect it, any more than they expect to be paid for the hospitality I always accept when staying among them. They expect to do these things for their foreign teacher, as for their own evangelists. Would I then be doing them a kindness to encourage a mercenary spirit where there is none to begin with?

So strongly did he feel about the idea of paying converts to preach the gospel, he called it a 'vicious system.'

It is the line of least resistance, but is something like the broad road that leads to destruction. No! far better let our work go slowly, and tread the narrow way of self-support. We shall never regret it . . .
What I want to see everywhere is the spirit of SACRIFICE for the Lord Who bought us with His blood — a desire to prove not what we can get but what we can give — and my heart burns as I write it.

There were situations, however, where he was not absolutely rigid. In a village called City Hill a young man wanted to come on a preaching trip with James, to learn more. James felt this would be useful to him when he returned and worked in City Hill again. James suggested to the rather unstable believers of the village that they should find about forty rupees to support his wife and family for the eight months of the young man's absence. They offered one rupee between them, expecting James to give the rest.

There was a time (he continued) when I should have been chary of pressing the subject any further, with people living in such poverty. But I know the Lisu better now, and so proceeded to give them a good

round reproof for suggesting such a meagre contribution. They did not much like it, naturally enough,
and some of them grumbled and argued against me
vigorously. But I stood my ground.

I pointed out that they were proposing to give to
the work of the Lord, who had given His life for
them, just about one-sixtieth part of the money they
usually spent on tobacco and betel-nut. I reminded
them that there was more than one among them who
had not yet broken off opium, and that a single
opium-smoker would burn away enough money
during the eight months to meet the entire need! They
could not deny that for a single marriage they would
spend eight hundred times the amount they had
suggested each family should give — if not a thousand
or two thousand times as much!

'Yes,' they argued, 'but we *have* to get wives. That
is a necessary expenditure.'

'Very well,' I answered, 'if you think so little of
preaching the Gospel, perhaps it is not necessary for
the young man to go at all.'

And there I left the matter, begging them to
reconsider it. The lad himself was disappointed and so
was his young wife, a nice, true-hearted girl, who
really wanted her husband to go and learn more. I
myself felt saddened, more than any of them, and
made it a special matter of prayer that they might be
brought to a better state of mind and heart.

That evening they seemed to have come round a
little, and eventually they made the following arrange-
ment. Three of the eight families concerned promised
to take the wife and two children into their homes and
support them for a month at a time. Two other
families gave a rupee each outright. This amounted
altogether to a contribution of seventeen rupees —
instead of one.

It was not all they could have done, by any means;
but not thinking it wise to press the matter further, I
paid the balance of 23 rupees myself. I made it quite
clear, however, that I did not want them to give
anything at all, if they did it grudgingly.

'No, teacher,' they instantly replied, 'we are glad to give.'

How different a spirit from the evening before! The Lord had been working in the meanwhile.

Government Handbook
The British Government in Burma asked James to produce a Lisu handbook. Feeling this would also help the work of mission, James went down to Tengyueh to work on it after his months at Turtle Village. There was no linguistic help and James found the task fraught with problems.

The first part of the handbook described the origins of the Lisu in Eastern Tibet and their migratory history and customs. The second part was a grammar, syntax and table of sounds. The third section was a Lisu-English vocabulary.

> You have no idea, James wrote to his mother at this time, how difficult it is to systematize a thing which has never been systematized before — in the whole history of the Lisu race, especially when you have learned it simply by ear, picking it up! It is impossible to force it into a European mould. You cannot make the grammar, for instance, fit in with the framework of an English or Greek grammar. Chinese and Kachin handbooks give the best suggestions, but there are so many things peculiar to the Lisu language that you have, more or less, to work out your own *system de novo.*

The handbook was published by the British Government in Rangoon in 1922, a little book of 108 pages.

A New Lifestyle for the Lisu
The coming of the Christian faith, James realised, was going to mean a whole new way of life for the

tribespeople. The use of their land, the beginnings of education, a new diet, a changed attitude to government, the coming of medicines; these were all aspects of life that needed thinking through. Obviously changes would come slowly, and practical advice would be needed.

James was absorbed in finding out about soils and agriculture. If the Lisu were not going to grow opium, what could their upland fields grow? How could their farming methods be improved to make their farms profitable?

> By the by (he wrote to his mother), do you remember my telling you of Forrest, the botanical expert who has spent some years in Yunnan, collecting specimens of orchids, rhododendrons, etc? He has just been here again, and I have been pumping him for all the agricultural information he could give me . . . He had been a farmer in Scotland and a fruit-grower in Australia before taking on his present work, besides which a man could hardly be a botanist and know nothing of agriculture, could he? I am glad to find that some of my own conclusions, derived from reading and inquiry among people of this locality, are not far out.
>
> Forrest says that much of the red soil of this plain and district is loam, not pure clay, and that there is a considerable amount of the same kind of soil in England. He says that the large waste area to the NW of our plain could be made to grow wheat, potatoes and other things, if properly handled, but that this soil lies in pockets of volcanic rock, which come near the surface in places. He thinks that sugar-beet would grow well in it, but no native here has ever heard of such a crop — though sugar is even more expensive than at home.

Forrest brought armfuls of orchids into the house at Tengyueh and he and James hung them on gutters and tree-stumps in a blaze of colour. Orchids and rhododendrons grew in great masses over the hillsides, flaming up towards the forests and rocky slopes above the Tengyueh waterfall.

Earning his Keep

While in Tengyueh doing his translation work, Bible-teaching and consulting experts on agriculture, James made a controversial move.

He wanted to support himself for the next few months by teaching two hours a day in the local boys' school.

This must have been a hot potato.

He had wanted to earn his own keep as Paul did by making tents, and when this opening came he managed to persuade Mr Hoste to agree to it. So for two hours every morning (7am-9am) he taught English in the school. This left him free for the rest of the day, and he sent to the Mission all he earned over and above the normal remittance. He kept receipts from Shanghai carefully.

> This will avoid the imputation of my making money on the side for myself (he wrote to his prayer helpers), and yet I shall have the delightful feeling of earning my own salt — working for the right to be a missionary, so to speak — and shall also have extra money to put into the printing of Lisu books, which is costly, hospitality to Lisu visitors, etc. It will tie me down somewhat, of course, except for the summer vacation in July, but I do not mind that just at present. I want to do literary and training work, which can be better managed here than elsewhere.

James sometimes commented on the dangers of Christian workers fitting less into their time than those in secular employment. Here he could earn more than

his keep by 9am, spend the morning on the Lisu
translation of John's gospel, the afternoon on a regular
Bible class for Lisu 'home missionary' students, and the
evenings on the Government Handbook. There was
always time for a walk with Forrest to look at soils and
agriculture.

Timetable Overturned
Just when James had settled down comfortably to
his translating, teaching, Bible studies and farming
interests, in walked Lao Luh.

Lao Luh was one of the two Lisu companions who
had gone with Allyn Cooke to the Cold Country. He
came in looking travel-weary after seven days of
climbing over the mountains, and had a badly
ulcerated eye. But he brought news of more and more
families destroying their demon-shelves and turning to
God.

While his eye was being treated Lao Luh told the
story of a Lisu lad who had been asked to come
eastwards across the Salween to explain the message of
Jesus Christ to waiting villages. The lad had gone
willingly wherever he was asked and at least a hundred
families had burned their demon-shelves and become
Christians. Now they sent urgently for more teachers
and for books.

So much for James's tidy timetable at Tengyueh!

The call of this new development was clear. It was
too pressing to allow him either to finish the school
term or his translation of John. Mr and Mrs Flagg felt
they should move the HQ to the Lisu mountains in the
Cold Country. Getting back and forth from Tengyueh
was a waste of time. James wrote home at this time:

> My young Lisu helper arrived in here three days ago
> (on April 11), and reported the 'turning Christian' of

over a hundred families in a new district just across the
Salween. The movement is still spreading there. Lao
Luh only came in because of a very painful eye (ulcer
on the cornea) which we are trying to cure. He says that
there were many more invitations from other villages
which he had not had time to accept.

Imagine what it is to have between five and six
hundred families (representing some three thousand
people) looking to you as father, mother, teacher,
shepherd, adviser etc. etc. It is a big responsibility.

You know (he added) that, rightly or wrongly, I
went in for big things when I took up tribes work: and I
do not regret it. I believe that to a large extent we get
what we go in for with God — only sometimes we have
mistaken ideas as to how it will come about.

Typhoid

Three stories came back into James's mind as he set off
with Ba Thaw to conduct a Bible convention at
Muchengpo for the hundreds of young believers of the
Cold Country.

One was of a booklet dropped in a puddle at the
Mangshih market and carried by a small boy to a
pastrycook in the Cold Country. It was from Moh's
home that the whole movement had begun, now
numbering thousands of believers.

Another memory was of a young American who
couldn't speak the language but who saw spiritual
realities clearly enough to weep. Allyn Cooke's tears
were the beginning of a work of God, a work which had
gathered its own momentum, and now the net was
almost breaking.

He also recalled an incident on the banks of the
Salween. Having crossed by ferry the previous year,
James heard two men calling from the side he had left.
Unable to hear them above the rushing waters, he
assumed they were calling the ferry, and went on his

way. He now learnt from Lao Luh that they had
wanted him to preach in their villages. These were the
people who had invited the Lisu lad instead, and this
was the harvest he was going to see.

How little active part James had played in all this;
but how much had his prayer forces done?

For two full weeks, morning, noon and night, the
Bible Convention continued. The people were hungry
for intensive teaching, and already seven voluntary
preachers from this new area had come forward. Ba
Thaw and Moh had plans to travel round the Shan
plains of the south after the convention, but James
somehow felt he should go back to Tengyueh.

Within a week he was at the gates of death. He
collapsed suddenly with typhoid fever and malaria. For
some weeks he tossed in raging, delirious bouts and
very nearly died. Mr and Mrs Flagg prayed for him,
nursed him and kept vigil, never sure if he would last
the day.

However, after repeated relapses, at last he was able
to write:

> I have any amount of things to be thankful for, and
> the first is that I just got back to Tengyueh in time. I
> calculate, now, that if I had gone down to Mangshih,
> the fever would have caught me two days' journey away
> from here, with no place to stay at, no one to look after
> me, no proper food or facilities for nursing in such
> serious illness. As you know, I have scores of times put
> to the test the simple plan of waiting upon God for
> guidance in perplexity, and have never yet been
> disappointed. Decisions so made have invariably
> proved to be wisest and best.
>   Flagg came down from Paoshan specially to look
> after me and has been nursing me ever since. Mrs
> Flagg moved out of their own room (the best in the
> house) to put me in it. They have given me the use of
> anything and everything they have . . . I am wearing

Flagg's dressing gown as I write this. Naturally I feel very grateful to them, and I am sure you will too.

It was a little insight into the unique fellowship there is among colleagues in the work of God.

HQ at 7,000 Feet

A little mission bungalow was built on the high slopes of the Cold Country above the Salween gorge. But when James got there he was still too weakened by his illness to stand the bitter winds and went down with pleurisy, his legs too swollen to walk. Although he had to spend Christmas Day in bed instead of enjoying the crowded Christian festival, he was heartened by the quality of life he already saw among these Lisu Christians.

> The Christians of three out of four of these Cold Country villages have been among the most satisfactory we ever had — so loyal, so hearty, active and intelligent.
> God will reward them . . . I think of one or two men, leaders in nearby villages, who have done almost everything they could possibly do for us, refusing any payment, and who say:
> 'Teachers, we ought by right not only to do what we have done, but to support you in food and clothing as well.'
> They remind me of what the Apostle Paul said of Aristarchus, Mark and Justus (Col. 4.11) — 'men that have been a comfort unto me.'

Three weeks' journey to the north a pioneer worker, Mr Lewer, was working among the people of the Upper Mekong and sent a request for two Lisu workers to help him.

Two volunteers were not hard to find. Leaving their farms and families to the care of the Christians they set off on a three-week trek over the heights to an

area they had never seen. They had no idea how many
months they would be away, nor was there suggestion
of payment of any kind. They would live on what they
could find in the mountains and what they were given
when they arrived. It was a good indication of their
spiritual calibre.

Travelling Magistrate

'I never made a more needed journey,' James wrote
after his next few months of travelling.

For three and a half months he had travelled alone,
acting as adviser, judge and teacher. In places, the
persecution of the young believers had been severe.
Some of the converts told James they really felt the
only solution was to get swords and cut their enemies'
heads off. There was a good deal of teaching and
pacifying to be done.

There were cases of abduction he was asked to deal
with too.

> A case has just come up which I am having to
> settle. A Christian girl was run off with by some
> heathen of the same locality. They tried to get her to
> recant and consent to be the wife of a heathen man,
> but she stuck to her guns bravely — and being afraid
> of getting into serious trouble with us, they let her go
> again. But, returned or not returned, we cannot let our
> girls be abducted with impunity and are taking the
> matter up. The Christians are very indignant about it.

Handshaking had become a Christian sign. When
James came to a village by invitation the whole
community would line up on each side of the approach
trail and shake hands — usually with both hands —
eyes shut and teeth clenched in their earnestness.

> The country is poor and barren (he wrote). The
> mountains are high and rocky, and the poverty of the

people terrible. Many, if not most of them, are in rags
and tatters, and the dirt of the hovels in which they
live makes it a trial to the flesh to be amongst them.

But he lived in their homes day and night and
noticed that for all their poverty they had already built
eight little chapels in the new area over the Salween.

Trying to reach as many of the two hundred or
more families as possible, James arranged a two-week
'teach-in'. The people loved anything in the nature of
a festival and came in crowds. The chief problem was
to get them to listen; they would happily talk to each
other and to him while he was trying to teach. Pigs,
chickens and toddlers added to the confusion and if a
herd of cattle passed the entire congregation would go
out to watch.

> Impatient with them? (he wrote). Well, now, let me
> whisper to you — yes, I am afraid I do get a little
> impatient, sometimes. But then, remembering the
> dense ignorance these people have been brought up
> in, the absolute lack of Christian nurture or advantages
> of any kind, one feels sorry ever to have been impatient
> with them. And they mean so well, too! You see them
> sitting there — men, women, boys and girls — in all
> their dirt, poverty and ignorance; you remember One
> Who was never impatient, never harsh, even with
> sinners and outcasts, and your heart melts to them
> again. You have a new understanding of what it
> means, 'He had compassion on the multitudes, for
> they were as sheep having no shepherd!'

He found, too, that they were all too concerned
about secondary and external issues. Could they eat
beans pickled in alcohol? Could they wash their
clothes on Sunday? These things preoccupied them
when James wanted to teach them more important
truths during his brief visits.

But when he compared the Lisu work with that of some Chinese towns, where living conditions were comfortable but the work was barren, he admitted that he loved to come 'right away up to these mountains, amid the rocks, mists and forests to find ourselves in little Lisu chapels of bamboo and thatch put up by simple Christian folk for the worship of God.'

James had a strong sense, borne out by events, that he was merely assisting in a work done wholly by God Himself. Time and time again he was invited to village chapels he did not know existed. No foreigner had been there, least of all himself.

The people are perhaps shivering through their rags. They are poor, dirty, ignorant and superstitious, but they are God's gift to us. You ask God for spiritual children, and He chooses them out for you. You shake hands with the brothers and sisters and mothers He has found for you, and sit down with them, the boys and girls all around you if possible. For I would far rather teach Lisu children to sing 'Jesus loves me, this I know', than teach the integral calculus to the most intelligent who have no interest in Christ.

For if two things stand out clearly in my mind (he wrote after this journey) they are firstly how 'foolish' and 'weak' our new converts are, and secondly that God has really chosen them. I Cor. 1. 27,28 is fulfilled before my very eyes! If you could come out here and see how useless mere preaching and persuasion is among these people, you would understand this better. One feels so helpless in face of their ignorance and need! But the Lisu work in our present district, with over two hundred families on either side of the Salween River (i.e. four hundred and more families in all) has been spontaneous from the beginning.

They will take you to a village you have never set foot in or even heard of before, and you will find several families of converts there, some of whom can read and write after a fashion, and a chapel already

put up! They just teach one another — inviting
converts over from neighbouring villages for the
purpose. They just want to be Christians, when they
hear all about it, and just turn Christian, missionary
or no missionary. Who put that 'want-to' into their
hearts? If they are not God's chosen, God's elect, what
are they?

No Time to Preach?

Years before, when James had been travelling on a
promised visit, a woman had called out and asked him
where he was off to.

'Just going up the mountain.'

'What for?'

To tell them about Jesus Christ. I am a preacher.'

'Well, stay and tell us about Him.'

'I haven't time just now.'

'What's the use of being a preacher if you've no
time to preach?' James remembered this. He
remembered the very spot where it happened. To his
astonishment, on his return to the area he found the
Lisu building a new mission HQ on the very site
where the woman had stood. With Flagg's help a new
station was being planned there because it was more
sheltered than the previous one.

It was almost finished when James saw it, complete
with a kitchen, goathouse and garden, and not a
penny would the Lisu accept for it all. Here at
Muchengpo, with spectacular views of the mountains
and unbelievably fertile soil a natural centre of the
work had been born.

> Here we are on a ridge (James wrote) protected on
> both sides by the slopes of a big deep valley, covered
> with forest . . . The vegetation is luxuriant and the
> effect superb as the clouds roll up over the hill-top or
> hang suspended half-way up the mountains. I like it

here: we all do. The Flaggs are thinking of putting up a permanent home next dry season . . . After a shower such as the one just over, the streams rise high. I can hear the roar of the river down in the valley below us, as I write. But the weather is wonderful for crops and gardens. Things seem to spring out of the ground almost as by magic, for the soil is fertile. Ferns and grass grow luxuriantly, and the trees are high. We are hoping great things from our experimental garden, having planted seeds from India and America, as well as yours from Letchworth.

One Sunday James watched Flagg baptise no less than 240 believers in the river below the chapel.

Stocktaking
Fourteen years had gone by since James's arrival in China. Life had been full of variety, even if mixed with extreme hardship. He had not thought of taking holidays very much — nobody did — but felt now it was time to apply for his first furlough.

In the days before he left, James did some stock-taking. He had learnt early and painfully the part tenacious prayer plays in the advance of the Kingdom of God. His reflections on the prayer of faith, from his tiny outpost high in the mountains produced a valuable document for his prayer-forces.

He now reviewed the state of the infant Lisu church, in some places muscular and perceptive, growing apace; in others, for all his days and days of teaching, falling back into spirit worship. Two of his most promising young men had reverted to it after months of careful nurturing.

'I used to think,' he wrote, 'that prayer should have the first place and teaching the second. I now feel that prayer should have the first, second and third place and teaching the fourth.'

Understandable criticism of James and his methods came from various observers. Why on earth did he take on so many areas at once? Wouldn't it be better to build up a few villages at a time? News was already coming in from Mr Lewer in the far north of the province of over a hundred families turning to God, right up on the Tibetan border. The work of God just seemed to go on spreading.

Some missionaries question whether my methods are the best. They feel that I am trying to cover too much ground, and that it would be better to go in for 'intensive work' as it is called . . . What is the use, they wonder, of spending two or three days in a village and then going on elsewhere and leaving them for perhaps a year? What can you expect of them? Why, they know practically nothing! Yes, I admit that it is not ideal. I believe in instructing my converts as much as any-body. Yet I can show numbers and numbers of Lisu Christians, with no more knowledge than two or three days' instruction could impart, standing firm *with the grace of God behind them* (that is what makes all the difference), trying in their blundering way to observe the Lord's Day, to pray and to sing — while those you give weeks and months of attention to, in other places, fall away.

Instruction, especially in the Scriptures, is a splendid thing. It is necessary, essential, if a man is to grow in grace. We are to be 'renewed unto knowledge after the image of Him that created him'. Paul prays for his converts that they may be filled with know-ledge. Knowledge is good, wholesome, needful. If a man is already a Christian, knowledge — spiritual knowledge — will help to establish him. I intend to do all I can to impart spiritual knowledge to my converts. I do not despise secular knowledge either. It is, I believe, a help rather than a hindrance to the apprehension of spiritual truth. But it is possible to over-emphasize almost anything, however good it may be. Paul believed it possible to over-emphasize knowledge, as his first letter to the Corinthian Church shows, in more than one passage. They say that 'knowledge is power'; but this, I feel, needs to be qualified. In the spiritual realm it is certainly not true that knowledge always imparts power to keep a man from falling away.

As a matter of fact, much knowledge has no life-giving power in it at all. I really believe it is possible to preach dead sermons — full of good, orthodox truth, but dead because the power of the Holy Spirit is absent. I believe it is possible to read a dead Bible, for the same reason. There is no magical charm about the letter of even God's Word. Apart from the power of God's Spirit, the best instruction we can give our converts is as dead as the dry bones of Ezek. 37. With the 'breath of God' breathing upon it, it may become as powerful as 'the exceeding great army' the bones were turned into. The power came from the breath of God, not from the dry bones. The dry bones were all right, but they were absolutely useless without the breath of God. And so is education, teaching, instruction of any kind out here on the mission-field, if it is of the dry bones variety. Some people go so far as to say that the problem confronting the church on the mission-field is fundamentally an educational one, and too many put that belief into practice. It seems to me like constructing costly artillery, firing big shells — and doing no damage to the enemy. And I can imagine Satan laughing up his sleeve.

World War I had been raging during part of James's term on his battlefield. He often referred to it in his letters. Comparing his own situation he wrote:

These people out here are not only ignorant and superstitious. They have a heathen atmosphere all about them. One can actually feel it. We are not dealing with an enemy that fires at the head only — i.e. keeps the mind only in ignorance — but with an enemy who uses GAS ATTACKS which wrap the people round with deadly effect, and yet are impalpable, elusive. What would you think of the folly of the soldier who fired a gun into the gas, to kill it or drive it back? Nor would it be of any more avail to teach or preach to the Lisu here, while they are held back by these invisible forces. Poisonous gas cannot be dispersed, I suppose, in any other way than by wind springing up and dispersing it. MAN is powerless.

For the breath of God can blow away all those miasmic vapours from the atmosphere of a village, in answer to your prayers. We are not fighting against flesh and blood. You deal with the fundamental issues of this Lisu work when you pray against 'the principalities, the powers, the world-rulers of this darkness, the spiritual hosts of wickedness in the heavenlies' (Eph. 6. 12).

I believe that a work of God sometimes goes on behind a particular man or family, village or district, before the knowledge of the truth ever reaches them. It is a silent, unsuspected work, not in mind or heart, but in the unseen realm behind these. Then, when the light of the Gospel is brought, there is no difficulty, no conflict. It is, then, simply a case of 'Stand still and see the salvation of the Lord'.

This should give us confidence in praying intelligently for those who are far from the Gospel light. The longer the preparation, the deeper the work. The deeper the root, the firmer the plant when once it springs above ground. I do not believe that any deep work of God takes root without long preparation somewhere . . .

On the human side, evangelistic work on the mission field is like a man going about in a dark, damp valley with a lighted match in his hand, seeking to ignite anything ignitable. But things are damp through and through, and will not burn however much he tries. In other cases, God's wind and sunshine have prepared beforehand. The valley is dry in places, and when the lighted match is applied — here a shrub, there a tree, here a few sticks, there a heap of leaves take fire and give light and warmth long after the kindling match and its bearer have passed on. And this is what God wants to see, and what He will be inquired of for us: little patches of fire burning all over the world.

8 LOVE STORY

Furlough in England

The family silver gleamed on the snowy cloth, and candles woke a hundred lights in the crystal glass. Dinner was a formal affair and Mrs Fraser presided with ceremony and aplomb. A quiet maid wheeled the trolley across the polished floors. Cook had been ordered to produce her chef d'oeuvres tonight to celebrate something of a family reunion: James had arrived home.

Generally Mrs Fraser ordered plain fare. She had pretty set ideas on what she regarded as a healthy diet. A piece of plain bread must be eaten with every roast dinner. A child should have only just enough to satisfy hunger: he should always leave the table feeling he could eat the whole dinner again. Small children were to have meals with servants in the kitchen until their manners were perfected for the dining-room.

However, Mrs Fraser indulged James's appetite for porridge, turnips and potatoes. 'The only place where I can eat unashamedly as much as I really want is at my mother's table,' he said.

There was a certain constraint at the reunion dinner.

'Well, James, you regret it now, don't you?' said a young voice. 'Throwing away your life in the back-woods, achieving precisely nothing.'

There was acid in the voice, and James did not reply. He was wounded though. Members of one's natural family could sometimes bring iron into the soul. They lived in another world.

But his mother's glance said a good deal. James's reunion with her had been memorable and moving. It wasn't long before she had brought all his prayer band to see him, talk with him and pray with him: the highlight of his whole furlough. He showed them his photographs, tribal costumes and Lisu ornaments. He told them his plans and hopes.

James was always full of bright ideas. He wanted a hand-wound record-player, good photographic equipment and, as he wrote to a relative, a radio outfit with a transmitting station at HQ in Muchengpo and receiving equipment in all Lisu villages.

> Then we can broadcast our preaching, teaching etc., all over our district . . . This is what you might call thinking imperially, isn't it — and it would probably need an imperial amount of money to get it going. However, nothing like bright ideas, is there?

This was 1922. He was a little ahead of his time.

In contrast to his visits to his prayer-band and sympathetic friends James had some disappointing meetings.

China seemed a long way off to some of his listeners: remote and mildly interesting but hardly related to their lives in any way. His story of the remarkable turning to God among the tribes was not of much importance, they seemed to say. No doubt he enjoyed travelling around helping these people.

Maybe James wasn't an exciting speaker. Perhaps he didn't convey his story well. At any rate, the lack of interest in his work during his furlough in England left a scar on his heart. He felt he had waited so long to share the news, but few people wanted to hear.

There were others, of course, who understood. They tried so hard to picture the terrain and its people and were able at least dimly to imagine it. But they grasped at once that God was at work among these tribespeople and they wanted to be co-workers with Him. Many of these James helped draft into the Prayer Companionship: ten soldiers in prayer standing behind each man on the field. This grew to be an army of thousands in the following years; intimate partners in the whole work of the mission.

Canada and USA

James's father was Scots-Canadian, and a large part of the Fraser family lived in Ontario. James's older brother, Gordon, had settled there with a business producing washing machines, and James combined a visit to his own relatives with a few weeks in USA. It was on this visit that he spoke at the Firs Conference, where Isobel Kuhn first heard about the tribes and felt God wanted her in the work. He took part in various conferences and meetings across the States and found a readiness to listen almost everywhere. People warmed to his story.

His closest companions in Yunnan had been largely Americans already, and as the team grew in later years, more and more of his colleagues were from the States. Partly because of this and partly because of his own nature he always had a special love for America and its Christian people. They were so warm, so generous and so dedicated, he said, so open to new ideas and initiatives! They were not afraid of being unconventional.

'If I had children,' James said, 'I should like them to grow up in America. And yet,' he added ruefully, 'get a British education!'

His last letter before leaving for the East was written from Vancouver in large excited handwriting:

> I reach Yokohama Sept. 8th, Shanghai Sept 12th, and Yunnan by the end of September. I say goodbye to civilisation now, feeling quite happy nevertheless. The whole crowd here will be down to see me off in the morning . . . I haven't started packing yet.

Shock

A bitter blow waited for him in Shanghai. Mission leaders planned to send him to North China for the next few years. Problems had arisen in Kansu and they wanted James's assistance there.

It was one of the greatest disappointments he had ever faced. Not that the decision was reached without a consultation. There simply wasn't anyone else to send. Besides, it would be good experience for James if he was to be drawn into the administrative side of the CIM.

'I can't say I'm willing, Lord, but I'm willing to be made willing,' prayed F B Meyer. James knew the barrenness of obeying reluctantly. Recognition that God's will was perfect and acceptable would be costly, but it was always fruitful, in his experience. He cast his mind back to the many disappointments he'd had in his plans for South-west Yunnan. There was the time Allyn Cooke, all ready and trained to join James in tribeswork — a colleague at last — was sent to the Chinese city of Tali.

'I was disappointed too,' Allyn admits. 'I stayed in Tali rebelliously for some months until I confessed my bitterness to God on my knees and asked Him to make me useful to Him in Tali. The very same day a letter came from HQ releasing me for the tribes.'

So James made a painful change of course and set

his face towards the vast plains and forbidding heights of Kansu. Determined to set his sails for the blessing of God, he learned to love the new province; but he was never able to forget how much it cost him. 'Yunnan was my first love, my Rachel,' he said, 'but Kansu became my Leah.'

Majesty and Terror: Kansu

Again you need to look at the map to understand something of the background to the story of the next few months.

Travelling and travelling: this was the pattern for three years, visiting mission-stations all over the vast open spaces of North-West China. The borders of Kansu stretch from the Gobi Desert to the Tibetan mountains.

James's travelogue makes fascinating reading. He was travelling on horseback through one of the least known and most forbidding areas of Asia. Desert plains gave way to bleak and towering mountains where blizzards blew with cutting teeth. Ghost towns left by Moslem wars stood silent but for the dusty wind and the occasional howl of a wolf. Hours passed as James and his Chinese coolie jogged along on their horses, with no sign of human life in any direction as far as the eye could see. Bleak deserts seemed to stretch to infinity, relieved sometimes by the Tibetan snows standing sharply against a black sky.

The cold was intense. His diary records:

> With thick underwear, a shirt, a woollen sweater, an undercoat, a fur-lined overcoat, a wadded gown and wadded coat on top you try to imagine you are warm . . . When a Kansu winter shows its teeth it's no joke to be out in it . . . Was bitten by a savage Kansu dog in the inn last night . . . Tibetan dogs are still

fiercer they tell me, and will follow you for miles.
They have been known to jump on a horse's back and
bite a lump of flesh out of it.

Sometimes there was no inn, so James and his
muleteer slept in the open, where the moonlight was
as bright as day. They ate dough-strings by a gipsy fire.
At least once they spent a night by a pass in the frozen
mountains at 13,000 feet. 'I don't know that I have ever
before spent a night at such an altitude.'

Caravans passed them at lonely points in the
heights, Tibetans driving their yaks, or Mongols on
mules, some from as far as Turkestan.

After a day's battle through a fierce blizzard James
wrote:

> You arrive at the end of the day cold, hungry and
> tired, not to find a nice clean room waiting for you, a
> warm bath, a warm fire, a smile of welcome and a nice
> meal! No, you splash along the slushy streets from
> dismal inn to dismal inn . . . and you get suspicious
> stares. Finally you practically force your way into an
> inn. It is pitch dark; the floor is a mess; there is no
> furniture but a mud platform, no light, no warmth . . .
> You and your muleteer make a meal of plain boiled
> rice.
>
> But next morning you get out again into your blue
> skies and snow mountains and forget all your
> previous night's troubles.

The Gifted Women

Headquarters had asked James for a survey of the
work in Kansu as well as a report on political unrest.

Faithful years of old-style missionary work had
been done on many a settled 'station'. Of one he
commented in a letter home:

> The church building is rather a handsome one,
> but — I am sorry to say — put up entirely with foreign

money. You remember my staying with Mr M-? well, it was he who donated the money for the building and it is he who supports the evangelists here. He is a generous and good man, like many similarly generous and good people at home, but I am more convinced than ever that it is a mistake to use foreign money on the mission field as we do.

Disturbed as he was by the state of the work in some places, James was fired with enthusiasm when he came upon Mildred Cable and Francesca and Eva French. Their whole lifestyle fascinated him.

A Dr Kao who pastored the church at Suchow had been thrown into prison on trumped-up charges and the three women asked James to help rescue him. Dr Kao was a fine preacher, 'but has no gift whatever for teaching,' James commented. The three women had arrived to evangelise the area, saw Dr Kao's need, and fitted into the work 'as a key into a lock' as he put it.

These women were first-class Bible teachers. James wrote:

I don't suppose we have in the whole of the CIM a more capable teacher than Miss Cable — of any subject. She was recently offered a position at the Shanting Christian University. The thoroughness with which she teaches the scriptures to Dr Kao's young men is almost appalling! She makes them go through the whole Bible — no skipping — Minor Prophets, Revelation, everything. You should see their voluminous note-books and the questions Miss Cable sets them to puzzle out for themselves. It is really quite remarkable that whereas so many of us common missionaries have been more or less satisfied with a superficial knowledge of the Bible in our Chinese Christians, here — right up in one of the remotest corners of China — you have a band of young men who are being grounded in the word of God as very few others are in any part of the country.

Their dinner table was a delight.

> I don't remember being at any missionary table
> where I have listened to such fresh and intelligent
> conversation — from the Great Pyramid to Einstein's
> Relativity. Miss Cable asks you what book you are
> reading and if you aren't reading anything wants to
> know why you aren't.

Dr Kao himself had daringly original ideas on how
church affairs should be run. He supported himself
with some medical work, but did not believe anyone
should be paid for anything he did for the Lord.
Anyone could share his house if they helped in the
work, but all were to provide for themselves. The
doctor was a deeply spiritual man. James spent many
hours with him in the prison, though was not to see
his release at the time, and felt his work was the
healthiest he had found in the province to date.

The doctor had a great heart for rescue work:
homeless and unwanted people found refuge on his
premises. He had literally dug his cook out of the
ground when he was being buried alive. One deaf and
dumb child James met was Topsy: still a child then.
'The poor child's legs had been bitten so savagely by
the dogs she could only just walk by holding on to a
wall,' he wrote. Left on the streets as unwanted, the
tiny child found a home with Miss Cable and later
became her adopted daughter.

James's years in Kansu and later Shensi came to an
end when all foreigners had to be evacuated during an
anti-foreign campaign which heralded the growing
Communist movement, in 1927. Europeans had to
leave the area quickly and face a hazardous journey to
the coast. James was one of a party which escaped on a
raft down the Yellow River, shooting the rapids, and
on occasions only just escaping bandits, until they

reached Shanghai. There they found that Europeans and Americans from many parts of inland China were converging, on consular advice: yet another rumbling from the earthquake later to expel foreigners altogether. It pressed home the need for urgency in the work.

Shanghai Interlude

'It's not light pleasure steamers skirting the coast we need,' D E Hoste said to James, 'but battleships to launch out into the deep.'

Hoste had plans to keep James, among others, at Shanghai to strengthen the central team. Exactly the same principles of faith and persistence were needed in the administration as on the Lisu mountains, the director argued. Now that he was forty, James's experience could be valuable in Shanghai.

Many mornings James joined D E Hoste's prayer-times. The need was colossal. There were places where Christian workers just couldn't get on with each other. There were places were all vision had been lost and no advance was ever made, or even expected. There were places where extremes of teaching resulted in splinter-groups, one after the other. There were still millions upon millions of Chinese who had never even heard of Jesus Christ. 'A million a month' were still dying in China without having heard the way of salvation, seventy years after Hudson Taylor first said these arresting words.

Although James spent some months at HQ he never felt God had equipped him for that side of the work. His heart was still strongly drawn to the people of South West Yunnan, and he felt his gifts and calling were for them. Yet he recognised the need. Who would not rather be out on the mountains than day after day in an office?

Mr Hoste thought it was high time James got himself a wife. His appearance sometimes left a lot to be desired. Surely there was a suitable lady to take him in hand? There was plenty of suppressed laughter behind the general director's door as Hoste suggested candidates to James.

As for scruffy appearance, James's principle was quite simple. 'When I'm in a strange place,' he confided, 'I think: it doesn't matter what I look like — nobody knows me here. If I am in a familiar place I think: it doesn't matter what I look like — everybody knows me here.'

He had no problem at all.

Reinforcements

It was now five years since James had seen the Lisu. When at last he could return, this time as superintendent of the province, he found a changed scene. Several young couples, almost all American, were now settled in among the tribes — the Kuhns, the Harrisons, the Fitzwilliams, the Castos, the Flaggs, the Gowmans and the Cookes. And more young workers were to follow.

His first year back on home ground was one of his happiest. He visited every area in the province where Christian work was going on, which meant he was able to see the fast-growing tribal churches. He was astonished to find large numbers of Christians high in the upper Salween, the area he had surveyed with Ba Thaw and Mr Geis fourteen years before. Carl Gowman had encouraged converts to evangelise almost at once and the message of the Cross had spread spontaneously further and further into the mountains.

Muchengpo already had missionary get-togethers, when Christian tribespeople met and read out letters sent by their own ambassadors. They sent them; they supported them; they prayed for them. It was a thought-provoking journey that James made when two Lisu came to Tengyueh to fetch him up the mountain trail to Moh's house in Hsiangta. Then they all set out together for Muchengpo, to one of the most moving welcomes James had ever been given. 'Elder Brother Number Three' had come back to them at last (number three because James was third brother in his family). James stayed three weeks with his people, a time not so much of teaching as of listening. The church had been growing in areas he hardly knew. The Cookes, the Gowmans and others had seen rapid expansion and were 'out of breath' trying to keep up with the Bible teaching.

A New Love
When Roxie Dymond's name was first mentioned, James's heart unaccountably turned over.

He had never heard of her before in his life, but immediately felt as if God had said something to him. Her name came up quite casually when he was talking to a friend in Kunming, capital of the province. Did James know, the friend remarked, that Frank Dymond of the United Methodist Mission had a daughter due to arrive in Kunming?

He saw her a few days later and his heart turned over again. She was only 23 and he was 42: surely this age-gap would be something of a hurdle? She belonged to another mission: could it be right for the superintendent of the CIM to marry 'outside his ranks'? In addition to all this, she was exceptionally pretty: fair and fragile, not built for his kind of life by the look of her.

And how could he engineer a meeting?

'Have you a piano in your house?' James asked Roxie's sister as casually as he could a few days later.

'No, I'm afraid we haven't.'

So that was no use. However, he could give a concert for all Europeans at the YMCA and make sure the Dymonds came. Invitations were sent out to all and sundry and along came the consuls, business-people, missionaries, and eventually Roxie, arriving late and squeezing in the back row. At the end she nodded her thanks and left.

It was obviously going to be very difficult to meet her. But the more he asked God to guide him about it all, the more he knew Roxie was the one for him.

He soon found a rendezvous, none too impressive for his bride-to-be. Roxie remembered it later.

> I can see it now: the tiled roof with the light streaming through the gaps, the draping cobwebs and the straight-backed Chinese chairs. Here he told me of his travels into Tibet and showed me photos of Ko-Ko-Nor and told me of the fierce Tibetan dogs which had attacked his horse. He told me of his travels in Kansu and in Yunnan, of his dearly loved mother and countless other things. Never once did he tell me of the way he had been used among the Lisu . . . He was a great conversationalist. He loved life and found the world full of interest. He had read widely, travelled widely and had a keen mind . . . He had a great sense of humour and few who knew him could forget the way he would throw back his head and laugh . . .
>
> One day he said, 'Roxie, I wish you were already my wife and this was our home.' I recall looking at the tiles, the gaps between the cobwebs and then at him, so gentlemanly yet so indifferent to comfort and material things. 'You know what my dream has always been,' he added with enthusiasm. 'Well, it has

been to have my wife on one mule, myself on another
and all my worldly possessions on a third.'

Roxie was attracted by his obvious strength and
manliness, but would the age gap be too great? Could
she cope as the 'Super's' wife? Could she manage all
this travelling?

James returned to his prayer and fasting. 'If you
will not have me,' he wrote to her, 'I'll go back to
being the loneliest man in China.'

Roxie's own father, Frank Dymond, had quite a
story to tell. He was only nineteen when he arrived in
China with the Methodists, and with his shock of red
hair and bright blue eyes the Chinese called him
'foreign devil' straight away. Frank and his friend
Sam Pollard braved inland China in times of fearful
hostility.

Born in China but educated in England, Roxie
graduated in history from Bristol University.

'I just couldn't make her out,' a fellow student said
recently. 'Roxie was in my year reading history. She
must have been the most stunning beauty in the
University. Men were always asking her to dances. But
she just didn't seem interested. Sort of preoccupied.
She never went.'

Christian student influences were strong during
these impressionable years of Roxie's life. She
admitted she hadn't much time or interest except for
Christian things. 'I seemed to have seen into another
world,' she explained later, 'and I could never be the
same again. I felt I was only a pilgrim here after that.'

Married Life
Planning a wedding in the backwoods of China was
quite an art. The usual trappings of a Western

wedding were not easy to get. The Chinese baker, for instance, was asked to produce a wedding-cake.

'We can't make a wedding-cake,' came the reply. 'Would a jam tart do?'

They were married in October, 1929. It was a golden day of sunshine and much laughter. The ceremony was held in a garden, to accommodate so many friends. James remembered it as one of the happiest days he'd ever known. Roxie had a letter from Mr Hoste wishing her well and 'envying her the companionship' she would enjoy.

There was no home for the bride. After only two or three days they set off on two weeks' journey to Tali, and then for several months among the mountains.

Roxie describes the experiences of early married life.

A few days after the wedding we started off for a five-and-a-half-month tour of reached and unreached tribes of west Yunnan. In those days west Yunnan was little known because there was no Burma Road and the caravan routes were over steep and rough, winding paths. At first I travelled by mountain chair, but soon changed to a mule, and for most of our travels we had two large mules to ride because they are more sure-footed than horses. When travelling in Chinese districts we usually slept in hay lofts of horse inns, and they often abounded in rats but were infinitely cleaner than ordinary inns. James was tremendously strong and frequently spent most of the day running along-side my mule, leaping over boulders and climbing up rocky places, talking and reminiscing to me by the hour. Living in the wilds as he had done, he had grown very indifferent to dress (which to his great amusement he had to change a little after marriage!), yet even when staying in places little better than pigsties he was always the gentleman. And wherever it was possible to muster some people, he would take out his hurricane lamp at night and preach to them. On his return he would always spend much time in prayer.

After weeks of travelling we reached the far west and James's old haunts among the Lisu. On reaching some of the villages we found guns fired in our honour, and shouts that 'Big Brother number three' was coming. I remember once travelling over the mountains for a very long day with hours of ascending and descending steep mountain slopes, reaching a Lisu village just as darkness was falling. After much handshaking and many greetings we had a crude meal and then proceeded to the little church for a service, which continued long after midnight. When I became overcome with sleep, I threw a pillow down at the back of the church and fell fast asleep, unnoticed. When I awoke I found that loving Lisu hands had put some fat pork and turnips on my pillow to gladden me when I opened my eyes!

The Lisu loved to sing, for they are very musical, and they were quick to learn four-part singing. They were full of life and humour, and there was a warm reality about their faith. Not only did they break with the gross sins of the past, but they were ready to take up the cross and follow their Lord. James constantly stressed with the Lisu in their early years of Christian experience our Lord's words, 'If any man will come after me, let him take up his cross daily and follow me.' This teaching was undoubtedly a source of great strength to them; many gave much out of their poverty, and some offered to lay down their lives to take the Gospel to the upper Salween.

For many weeks we travelled with the Lisu into new areas. Usually we camped out at night near a stream or other source of water, just lying down under the stars. Life was very simple. The Lisu carried rice, and with their own bows and arrows shot any birds, monkeys or squirrels they could find for meat. Crossing over into the Shan states of north Burma we travelled through the country of the Wild Wa. These people are much feared by the Chinese because they are head-hunters, but the Lisu carry poisonous arrows which the Wa greatly fear because they cause agonizing death.

Many of the people had never seen foreigners before. I remember them putting a stool on the hillside for me to sit on so that they could come and look at the first white woman they had ever seen. Travelling back through the south of the province, we spent eighteen days passing through tribal villages and Chinese towns where there was not a single mission station or witness for Christ at all.

They spent Christmas at Muchengpo, where hundreds of Lisu came for the festival and where the largest team of foreign helpers so far were engaged in intensive teaching, advising and consolidating. The expansion was almost entirely in Lisu hands, and it was not long before leaders and teachers also emerged from the Lisu church. Emphasis was laid over and over again on the temporary nature of foreign help. 'Don't stay anywhere too long,' James advised foreign workers. Looking back today, and knowing how soon all foreign workers were to leave it is clear that the Spirit of God directed the work from the start.

Allyn Cooke remembers James's advice to him to move on from Luda. 'You have compassed this mountain long enough (Deut 2. 3)' James told him. 'The people are beginning to depend on you.'

When we had gone, Allyn writes, recalling the event in 1981, the Luda folk began to manage their own affairs and trust the Lord more fully. They become much stronger by not having a missionary in the village . . . The Lord raised up leaders from among them and they began to reach out after the unsaved. Mr Fraser was definitely led by God in his advice to us. His views about self-support, self-government and self-propagation were what God used to make a

strong church which exists to the present time, with
no missionary living among them.

It was during the five months 'honeymoon' journey
that James and Roxie found the Cookes running a
Bible School for over a thousand Christians at a new
station at Fuhinshan. For a fortnight the two couples
shared a house perched high on a mountain ridge
commanding panoramic views of the dark ranges
between the Salween and Mekong Rivers. James was
able to help Allyn and Leila with the intensive Bible
Teaching, while Roxie tried hard to pick up what she
could of the language, knowing only Chinese.

It was during their 35 days' journey eastwards to the
Red River that Roxie saw the extent of the need for
Christian mission. Some of the trail was over a wild
expanse of empty mountainside, but their route also
took them through teeming cities and countless
villages which had never been visited with the message
of Jesus Christ. In fact Roxie's initial impression of
the work in West Yunnan was less of the crowded
chapels than of the hundreds of thousands yet to be
reached.

Whenever there was a chance James and Roxie took
their lamp out in the evening and preached to the
people in Chinese. Roxie had a voice that carried, and
she was a very gifted preacher, easily able to draw a
crowd. James felt preaching was more her gift than his
when it came to the Chinese.

Back in Kunming, capital city of Yunnan, James
was able to make something of a survey of the work.
He was not only involved in the mountains of the
south-west now. The Chinese cities claimed a big
share of his interest and responsibility, though as yet
they had been very much less ready to listen to the

message of Christ. Meanwhile the tribeswork still showed a steady growth, as he wrote in a letter soon afterwards.

Mr Cooke, now on the Upper Salween, has just sent an SOS for more volunteer evangelists from this district — fourteen days' journey away — as they have more and more families turning from demon-worship all the time. You will be interested to know that for the very first time in the history of this work we are about to send out three young women to teach in the villages near here. They are aged 16, 20 and 21. They have volunteered together, and seem to be so thoroughly in earnest that Fitzwilliam and I and the local deacons have decided to give them a trial . . . We are placing them under the direction of one of the regular Lisu evangelists and his wife . . .

I would like you to have seen them come into my study so bashfully and girlishly — two of them only on the excitedly whispered persuasions of the boldest of the three. And they all sat there for some time, mildly squirming before saying what they had come about. But they were so evidently in earnest. Perhaps you will pray for them sometimes. Their names are Tabitha, Sarah and Ruth . . .

You will know, doubtless, that Lisu work is entirely self-supporting. All the money for our regular evangelists, with their food and the food for their families, is provided by the Lisu themselves, from their harvest festival offerings. The volunteer evangelists are not paid at all, nor their families; but they are fed by the people in the villages they stay at. The work is largely self-governing also. All important matters are settled by the deacons of the whole district, at their annual meeting each December. There is also an Annual Meeting of the deacons of this district . . . usually presided over by our ordained Pastor Paul. This often partakes of the nature of a legislative assembly! They make rules, take minutes of the meetings, etc., whether the missionary is there or not.

I would love you to hear our Lisu singing. Mr and Mrs Cooke, our missionary musicians, have always taught them to sing in parts — and they do, with no organ either. It is really inspiring, and has often brought tears to my eyes . . . I have heard very few congregations at home, either in England or America, whose singing is so inspiring. They themselves love it. How you would like to go to bed on Sunday night to the strains of some sweet hymn tune which they are still singing, and in parts, in one of their homes in the village near by!

Oh, how I love to hear them sing, 'when my life-work is ended, and I cross the swelling tide!' I must not seem to boast — but I know one poor missionary heart that has swelled with emotion and praise, listening to the hearty and tuneful singing of these aborigines of the Burma-China border.

9   OIL AND WINE

A Night Alone

'You can fend for yourself now. We've carried these children far enough.'

The Chinese coolie dumped the baby on the grass and called his companion.

'We want our money now.'

'But you agreed to carry the load up the mountain', Roxie protested.

'We've changed our minds. We want our money now'.

Roxie counted out the money and handed it over. She stood staring at the men as they ran off down the trail. Before her, mountains rose silently against the sky. There wasn't a house in sight in any direction and night was falling fast.

The desolation of the scene overcame Roxie for a moment. She stood and prayed silently and waited. She had been travelling for five days already with her two little girls, and had found the Chinese coolies trustworthy and friendly. Their sudden decision to abandon her came as a complete surprise.

The purpose of the journey was to find James, who had gone down with typhoid in a Chinese inn. Although a fellow-missionary was with him, Roxie had set out to find him after weeks of waiting.

A few yards from the path Roxie found a small gulley where overhanging branches would make some protection from the rising wind. At least, she thought, the children will have some shelter for the night. She wrapped the baby up, put her in a corner by the rocks and went back for the bedding and packages. She could unpack the food and give the whimpering child something to eat.

About an hour later darkness had fallen completely. The children, mercifully, had gone to sleep; they were used to sleeping anywhere.

Suddenly Roxie heard voices and saw a lamp swinging down the trail.

The Lisu runners had come to find her.

They had heard she was on her way to find James and had volunteered to come and meet her, knowing nothing of her dangerous situation.

'I could have hugged them', Roxie said later. 'They carried the children and the stuff up the trail as if they were their own property'.

It was one of the many times God proved how much He cared about the little family and how much their well-being was His concern.

Jonathan Goforth

James couldn't shake off the effects of his illness for at least two months. He had obviously been weakened by all the travelling and the responsibilities attached to being superintendent. It seemed high time to go home again to England and the USA for a break after another nine years in China.

For one thing he wanted his mother to see his wife and two little girls. He had written so much about his children: one born in Shanghai, and the other, two years later, in Burma. He had always wanted girls — so much so Roxie was in fear in case the first, at any rate, might be a boy. Famed among the Lisu for his love of children — 'they were always climbing all over him', says Allyn Cooke — his own children were a constant joy and amusement.

In 1934, on her 79th birthday, his mother saw his family for the first time. James, she thought, looked older and tired. It was the last time she was ever to see him.

After some months in England, speaking at meetings all over the British Isles, James and his family left for North America. It was here that James and Roxie had a memorable experience.

They had heard of Jonathan Goforth, of course. He was a Presbyterian from Canada who had seen an unusual demonstration of the Holy Spirit's power in the northern provinces of China: Honan, Manchuria and right across to Korea. As early as 1906 crowds of Chinese had come to accept the message of the Cross and put faith in Christ through Goforth's preaching. More than this, Christians came into a deeper knowledge of God wherever he went.

James and Roxie went to a meeting where he was speaking in Canada in 1935. Goforth was by this time 76 years old and completely blind. When he stood up to speak there was such an unusual sense of the presence of God James and Roxie were stirred.

'Not by might, nor by power, but by My Spirit saith the Lord of Hosts'. This was Goforth's special emphasis. Wherever this man of God went, conviction of sin seemed to follow. The story he had to tell opened up a whole world of new possibilities and exposed a whole world of acute need among Christians. Thousands of people came into a new spiritual dimension through his ministry.

The meeting left an indelible impression on James and Roxie.

Administration

'There is a flame of a burning bush in everything that is a work of God', James said.

He felt this about office work in a special sense. When he arrived back in at headquarters he found himself detained there again. For many months James was typing letters in Shanghai.

The fact that he did not agree to stay permanently in any position there was because he did not feel this was God's will for him. It seems likely he was right.

He had some pretty independent views on mission. Isobel Kuhn generously states that he was simply '50 years ahead of his time'. But not everyone thought so. He tended to upset traditional applecarts, however gently he pressed his opinion. He had a good deal of criticism from some quarters, amounting to mild rebellion in one or two areas of Yunnan.

James never minded criticism. 'They are entitled to their opinion and I am entitled to mine', he said. The problem came, of course, when he felt indigenous methods — for example — *must* be adopted. This caused strong reaction sometimes.

Another of his views was on woman-power. He observed that women workers outnumbered the men yet a large proportion occupied themselves in house-keeping and secondary affairs, each in her home. Why not have communal meals, Kibbutz-style, and free all these women to preach and teach? People used to complain that the CIM got more than its fair share of gifted women. Were they really used as God had planned?

His own idea of married life was of an equal yoke, both partners in the work together. He wanted Roxie to travel with him and preach with him. He would happily go down to the river and wash the clothes or carry the baby on his back. It was a companion and co-worker he had always longed for, not a housekeeper. But he had to accept that this view was not shared by everyone.

Unfortunately, while James enjoyed discussion on all these things he found some peoples' 'hurtability' level very low, and they could nurse a grievance for a very long time. And this, he was quick to see, was a serious situation. Unity of spirit was vital to the work. Over and over again James made long journeys of several days, not to preach or teach, but to restore fellowship with a worker who was in dissent. No principle, he felt, was more important than that one. Perfect love among Christian workers was more vital than evangelism, if the two could be separated at all.

The dependence of mission on the spiritual state of the missioners was borne home to James early in his superintendency of Yunnan. As personnel increased, varieties of background and outlook multiplied. Endless opportunities for the clash of personalities presented themselves, especially in work at such close quarters. Unless there was victory here, there would be no victory anywhere else.

James thought a great deal about all this. Did God have something more for His people that they were not fully appropriating?

When God Works
During the 1930s various parts of China, especially in the northern provinces, had a touch of revival which had quickened the spiritual life there. The Bethel

Band (Andrew Gih and John Sung among others) visited Shansi in 1931 and rumours reached Shanghai of certain extremes of teaching beginning to circulate. James was asked to go to the Yutaoho Convention in Shansi in 1935, soon after furlough, to evaluate — and possibly even to steady — the tendencies to emotionalism or 'strange fire' which might be there.

Yutaoho summer resort was in a beautiful valley of water-mills. They stood one after another along the river bank where their wheels had been turned by the waters; but now they were summer houses for the missionaries.

Here James met a group of Christians open for all the blessing of God. Prayer-meetings often lasted into the early hours of the morning. There was a powerful sense of the Presence of God. James was one of the speakers and took as one of his themes 'The Fullness of the Holy Spirit'. Clearly he felt himself one in spirit with these people: they had unmistakably met with God. James described his week here as 'the happiest week of my China experience'.

Because this influenced his thinking and praying about his own work — and the Lisu in particular — it is worth noticing the character of this revival movement. It is summed up in a letter James kept with him, written after an earlier conference in Shansi. The writer wanted to show how, although many people at the conference had been missionaries for years, *everything* in their Christian experience changed when God came in power. It was no temporary excitement; it was a permanent change of course. The letter says:

From the outset the Lord began to pour out His Spirit upon us. The manifestations were according to Scripture.

1) *Conviction of sin* (John 16.8). Things that normally were winked at appeared exceedingly sinful when the Spirit of holiness threw His searchlight on our hearts, and there was confessing and putting away of sin.

2) *Revelation of Jesus* (John 16.14). What glimpses were given us of the grace and glory of the Lord! His Cross became more precious. His resurrection and mediation more real and His coming again a vital truth and purifying hope.

3) *Understanding of Truth* (John 14.26; 16.13). Our spirits were gripped by truths that hitherto had only reached our minds — what we had preached as theories we experienced as facts — Never have I known the definiteness and directness of the Spirit's teaching as in these days.

4) *Outpouring of Love* (Rom 5.5). We had thought we loved each other, and did up to a point, but when the Spirit of God revealed His standard, 'that they may be one as We are', we bowed in shame. (There follow accounts of brokenness, confession and new love between colleagues).

5) *Anointing of Power* (Acts 1.8). That the Lord has fulfilled His promise in the lives of some of His children is not now a matter of fond hope, but an obvious fact.

James had an increasing heart-hunger for God to do this among Christians in Yunnan. During the next few years this burden never left him.

Over the Christmas following the Yutaoho Convention James arranged three days of meetings for missionaries at Kunming. The theme of the little convention was The Holy Spirit: His personality, presence and power. There was a new depth in the meetings, a new seriousness of purpose.

'He spoke about a life in the Holy Spirit', wrote Mrs Cooke, 'as a blessing we should claim. He showed how in life after life in the Old Testament *an added blessing* was given, lifting it to a higher plane. So there is ever new and deeper blessing for us as we definitely receive the Holy Spirit. It has been so with me since then — daily victory that I never knew before'.

Another wrote: 'It was Fraser's zenith. He was a Spirit-filled man'.

James had already observed the contrast between the work of man and the work of God in church affairs. During these last years of his life he had a new pressure: a sense of the brevity of time and the immensity of the task. There was only one clear answer. Dr Lloyd-Jones says in his book *Authority*. 'Men have testified that they have learned more of God and of the Lord Jesus Christ in an *hour* in a meeting during a revival than they had learned in a lifetime of Bible Study and reading theology'.

Mountain Shanty Home

When Roxie arrived at Mrs Fitzwilliam's bamboo house in Kachin mountain country, she stood looking into the one downstairs room. Peering into the dark she was surprised to see two legs come through the ceiling followed by the bulky form of a Kachin woman who landed on the floor in front of her.

'Mrs Fitz' wasn't at all surprised.

'I keep telling her not to tread on that part of the floor up there and she forgets. She's always coming through'.

However, the house they planned to share was to be single-storied. James described it in a letter to a friend.

Mrs Fraser and the children are with the Fitz-williams. It would interest you very much to see them all living as they are in a bamboo house, single-storied, with a bamboo floor and thatched roof. They have a large garden in a most beautiful spot on the mountains, with Kachin villages all round (also Lisu, Palung and Chinese) and the plain of Chefang some six miles below. Longchiu in itself is an Atsi-Kachin village, about ten miles from the border of Burma . . . The headman and all his family are Christians, also several other families . . . making about ten in all. It is a small beginning, a door ajar rather than wide open, yet sufficient to give us a good entrance.

I will not go into detail as to how the Lord seemed to make the way plain before us — how we found the framework of a house exactly the size we had wished, all ready waiting for us; how it was in the best yet unoccupied site in the village, belonging to the Christian headman, who at once granted us permission to use it and live there; how we prayed-in the thatch for the roofing (we were too late to get thatch in the ordinary way); how the Christian Lisu in the village of Palien, three miles away, came and roofed our house without the cost of a penny; how we got the carpenters and finished all the necessary work in an unusual spell of fine weather, just before the rain set in, etc. etc. All this is the romance of missionary life to those of us who are in it, small details though they may seem.

There were three rooms: a Fitz family room, a Fraser family room and a common room. And from this base James came and went, while Roxie occupied herself with the Kachin work.

It was an idyllic spot in the mountains for children: a kind of permanent picnic. Plenty of goat's milk, plenty of eggs, always bowls of rice with 'Marmite gravy' — and mountains around as far as the eye could see. They had the winds and the sun up there, and when the rain came sweeping down the slopes they could go indoors and read about Peter Pan or Winnie the Pooh. When their library wore thin James composed a series of stories for them himself about a little girl called Pollyanna Pumpkin.

His fiftieth birthday was spent here, and the following months were full of journeys around the province. Sometimes he came back to find the Fitz family were away and Roxie and the children alone among the Kachin.

Monsoon

It was around this time that James was caught in a monsoon downpour and nearly lost his life.

Rain was sheeting down in front of him as he came over the border mountains. He had often been out in monsoons before but this rain was nearly heavy enough to knock a man off his horse and so deafening he didn't hear his Lisu companions calling.

Suddenly he found himself sinking. He leapt off his horse thinking he must be in the river, but felt a cold suction closing in on him and dragging him down. Under the surface of water there was a deep and lethal swamp. He found himself sinking down into it and was powerless against the suction. The mud had nearly closed over his head when he felt hands grabbing him. His Lisu companions had been quick to act, swimming on the mud as if it were water and keeping horizontal.

It was a desperate struggle to get him out, but finally he made it to the rocks. His horse was never seen again.

Lisu New Testament

It was a great day when news came that Allyn and Leila Cooke had finished translating the Lisu New Testament. It had been a mammoth work and completed at great cost to themselves. James was asked to come up to Luda and help with its revision. It was then to be typed (largely by Homay, a Lisu girl whom the Cookes had taught) and photo-printed in Burma. Leila Cooke wrote of James:

> He spent several weeks with us at Luda, and we covered every verse as far as Hebrews, working with him daily. But his help with the translation was not the only help we received. His daily messages for morning prayers were an inspiration . . . His capacity for work was astonishing but with it all he always seemed fresh and full of life, always of an even temper, always considerate of others, and a perfect gentleman.
>
> Our home life was greatly enriched through his coming. He had read widely, and his conversation was rich and varied. He would sit, between whiles, and play on our little organ — Chopin's Polonaise and treasures from Beethoven — bringing such glorious music out of it! The Lisu would crowd in to listen.
>
> And one thing that impressed me as the months went on — he had such wonderful control over every part of his life. He was completely master of himself. He not only wanted to live a self-denying life, enduring hardness for Christ's sake, he could do so. To bring his life up to his highest thought seemed to be quite natural with him. And he was so practical about it.
>
> His correspondence, for example, was very heavy. I have known him to sit up all night, answering letters. He would not let it interfere with regular hours of revision work during the day. When the mail came in, he would put the letters to be answered into envelopes addressed to the senders, and keep them on his table ready for attention.
>
> He was very sociable. When he wanted to write letters or study, he would come down and do it with us, rather than stay up in his room alone.
>
> No matter how busy he was he never cut short the morning time of family worship. He would often continue with us in prayer and Bible study until nine or ten o'clock. Mr Cooke and I were alone with him for a while, before Peterson and Carlson joined us, but Mr

Fraser was just as willing to impart his precious messages to us as to a large company. How we did enjoy them, for we had been long away from such ministry in our own tongue.

Hymn-singing was always part of these times of worship. Mr Fraser always chose the grand old-time hymns, and seemed so in his element — playing the little organ and leading us in song. His favourite hymn was: 'The Lord's my Shepherd, I'll not want,' and he would announce it by saying 'Let us sing a hymn written three thousand years ago.'

There were already over a thousand Christians at Luda. There had been some bitter persecution of them in earlier years, but the church had matured and expanded.

James loved the translation work. 'What fascinating work it is', he wrote to his mother. 'How I love Bible Translation and Bible teaching — and how both seem to water my own soul!'

Moses, the Lisu collaborator, knew almost all there was to know about Lisu tones and idioms. James's knowledge of Greek was scholarly. The Cookes were experienced translators, and when Peterson and Carlson came there was still more expert help.

They sat out in the sun of the mountainside during the day, looking up from time to time at the sweeping panorama below their position at 6,000 feet. When the evening brought a cold wind they would move the little table indoors by the fire.

Roxie brought the children after a few weeks, and the family moved with the translators to Oak Flat where the Kuhns had been stationed — they were now on furlough. Leila Cooke willingly looked after the children from time to time while James and Roxie went to the little bamboo chapel to spend time — sometimes hours — in prayer. It was not out of the sense of duty, but out of a sense of need, that they wanted this time for prayer. Surrounded as they were by Lisu Christians on all sides — a mighty answer to prayer in itself — they were aware of a need for a deeper work of grace in the Christians. 'Whoever is justified,' to quote Wesley again, 'has the choice of walking in the higher or lower path . . . to aspire after the heights and depths of holiness . . . or decline into the lower order of Christians.' James's prayer for these believers was that they might be 'filled with all the fulness of God.'

The completion of the Lisu New Testament, in what came to be known among translators as the 'Fraser script' was the fruit of years of hard work from that little band of labourers. James was less involved in it than some of the others, but shared in the excitement of the finished product. The initial publication was paid for by Christians in Manchuria.

The whole Bible wasn't available. in Lisu until 1968, and it was still later before the tribespeople could actually have them in any quantity. But the Lisu tribe became one of the leading Christian groups in this part of Asia largely because they could read and study the word of God for themselves.

Anna Christiansen

Knowing that the winds of God had been blowing in other parts of China, James wanted very much to see revival come to Yunnan. The sleep of death had settled over some of the Chinese Churches. They kept going, he said, 'but only just.'

He had heard a good bit about a Danish lady, Miss Anna Christiansen, and the remarkable effect of her ministry among the Chinese. She had been to Yunnan before, but now James wanted to arrange a series of conventions for her in Chinese churches.

She came in the spring of 1938.

Miss Christiansen's message was very plain and very straightforward. It was about sin in the believer: blatant sin, covered sin, secret sin. The Holy Spirit so used the message that wherever she preached 'great fear seized the whole church' (Acts 5.11). Roxie remembered later how some professing Christians trembled from head to foot. Even telling of these days years afterwards, she recaptured something of the sense of awe everyone had felt at the time.

> Things were uncovered in the church that we had known nothing about. Leading people wept and confessed the most terrible sins. It was as if the lid had been taken off. Many Christians realised for the first time that God will not be trifled with. The sense of His Presence was overwhelming. I had never seen people so pale and so shaken. The Holy Spirit brought into sharp focus the truths of sin, righteousness and judgement. People cried out in the name of Jesus for a heart made clean. Can you imagine the joy and boldness that followed?

One of the results was that lukewarm believers suddenly came into a powerful liberating assurance that they were born of God. Charles Peterson was there at the time. He writes:

> Souls came into a new relationship with God; wrongs were righted; sin confessed and many received assurance of the new birth. Great blessing came also to the Lisu who heard her . . . Job's heart was greatly stirred. He was certainly 'born again' before that time, but the truth had not gripped him. After that it was different. He returned to Padé, and during the April Bible-study week urged all the teachers to make sure

that they had the new birth. The blessing did not stop
there but was carried into Rainy Season Bible School.
During that time the evening services for an entire
week were concentrated on that subject and each of
our students was required to take it in the practice
preaching class. Their hearts were full of it, and
through them the blessed truth has been taught
throughout all the Padé district.

Six days southward of Paoshan, blessing came to
the Lisu at Menga (where Mr and Mrs Payne were
stationed) through another of Miss Christiansen's
missions. There were at least thirty Lisu there, and all
of them received help. Teacher Luke's experience is
typical. After hearing a message on covered sin, he got
a huge piece of paper and made a list of all the sins he
had ever committed, as far as he could remember.
Then he wrote at the bottom:

'But I have confessed them all to Jesus. He has
forgiven them and washed my heart. I know that I am
born again.'

Through these meetings blessing was carried to
most of our southern Lisu districts, and more than six
months later our Lisu are still speaking of Miss
Christiansen and the blessing they received at the
meetings she conducted.

Travelling on mules or sedan-chairs and sleeping
on piles of straw in wayside inns, Anna, James and
Roxie with their younger child (the older now at the
Chefoo school) went to place after place during the
following weeks witnessing similar scenes. Roxie
remembered thinking: it may not be the same at the
next place — they have special problems, they will be
hard to move. But in every place Anna's message,
accompanied by simple pictures of black, red and
white hearts, had the same dynamic effect. Conviction
of sin followed wherever she went.

Dan Smith was a young missionary at Tali when
Anna Christiansen came to the city and he

accompanied the party on some of their travels. He recalls in his autobiography the difficulties Anna herself faced. She was of a heavy build and unused to the ruggedness of mountain travelling. Her heart began to trouble her on one of the journeys so a sedan-chair carried by Chinese coolies was found for her. But the weight was too much for the coolies and one night they stole away, leaving the party stranded in a desolate, uninhabited area. After a long delay Lisu carriers were found. Being unused to carrying sedan-chairs they needed a great many more coolies to manage it at all, and between them they managed to give Anna one of the most frightening journeys of her life.

Yunnan had really come on the map with the opening of the Burma Road. The motor road now ran from Shanghai to Rangoon. But as the Japanese war with China intensified, the British insisted on a three month closure of the road into Burma. This led to anti-British feeling on the border.

One day Dan was escorting Anna when a young Chinese officer arrogantly accosted them. Were they English?

'I'm from Denmark,' replied Anna.

'Where's that.'

'It's a little country over-run by Nazis.'

'And you?' turning to Dan, 'where are you from?'

'My family came from Scotland,' said Dan.

'Where's that?'

'It's a little country over-run by the English.'

'So! We are all oppressed peoples. Come and eat with me.'

James had done most of his travelling alone during his journeys in South-west China. But during these trips with Anna's party Dan Smith was able to observe the older man in all the inconveniences and discomforts of the journey.

> Mr Fraser was a gentleman to his finger tips. There was nothing of lightness or flippancy. Wisdom governed him and every propriety was observed. I remember how often these things struck me when we journeyed together with Miss Christiansen. He was the perfect gentleman in the dirtiest and dingiest Chinese inns. Ask Miss Christiansen. She marvelled at the man. So did I. Every courtesy was observed. Every kindness was done. The depth of his inward life in Christ was never more manifested than in his attention to those hundred and one little things which make comfort for others.

The adventures and discomforts of the journey in no way sapped Anna's spiritual strength. Her simple message had a remarkable effect in the evening meetings. James wrote of her visit to Kunming:

> Miss Christiansen's meetings here were much blessed, and many came through to salvation who have never had a clear Christian experience. We had daily congregations of about 350 people nearly filling the chapel. Some, both foreigners and Chinese, came from other missions in the city — CMS, Methodist and Pentecostal. Perhaps the chief results were seen among the girls of the German sisters' Blind school and Slave Refuge. Some of these were so distressed over their sins they could not eat.
> Some dreadful sins were confessed, and by those of whom it had never been suspected. It is the same wherever Miss Christiansen goes. It is nothing but the power of the Holy Spirit, and she does not mince matters when she preaches on sins: the result showing that plain speaking was called for. It is John Wesley's method, and the method of every gospel preacher who aimed at and won definite repentances.

This was not revival on a large scale. But it was a token sign of the power of God. These meetings produced a lasting effect both among the Chinese and the tribespeople. They contributed to a spiritual experience which stood the test of time and much suffering. Within twelve years hundreds of believers in South-west China were to face prison and death for the faith. They will be among those 'who have come out of great tribulation but have *washed their robes and made them white* in the blood of the Lamb' (Rev. 7.14).

Travelling Light
James was beginning to feel that a province the size of Yunnan was too much for one man to supervise. Headquarters in Shanghai agreed with him that east and west of the province needed separate oversight, and advised James to look after the western half: his home territory. This would cut down a great deal on the time spent travelling, and give him the chance of a little more home life.

He planned to make a home in Paoshan. There was a telegraph office there; it was on the Burma Road; best of all he was still near the tribespeople. He had a secret hope that he might be able to help with Bible teaching up in the mountain churches again as soon as the printed New Testament came through.

But until the Paoshan home was arranged James was still travelling. He writes home a graphic account of one of his last journeys, from Paoshan to Tali, typical of the experiences of any traveller in China at the time:

> I am travelling just now by hired animals as, you remember, my own two mules died eighteen months

ago from foot and mouth disease. I wonder if you would be interested to know how I travel now . . . I will give you a specimen day.

I am in a tiny mountain village of about two or three houses . . . I have been sleeping soundly up in a loft reached by a short ladder, over the stable. My camp bed is quite a boon (I never used one before I was married). I rise at day break, hear them sizzling the fried vegetables downstairs, then get up to see if the muleteers are up and about. The distance between Tali and Paoshan is about as far as London to Sheffield but over ten times more mountainous country. They take eight days to do it as a rule; I am making them do it this time in six. I ride on one mule and put all my things on the other. In time the muleteers get up. We have the same food every meal which is always 1. Boiled or steamed rice. 2. A kind of slightly bitter dark green cabbage-like vegetable of which I am very fond. 3. Two fried eggs. 4. If possible a tiny bit of Chinese pickled beans. Then a little cup of Chinese tea or hot water. It suits me fine.

In due time we have had our breakfast . . . and we are off. Not perhaps before 7.0 a.m. when the sun is up. My bedding, in which I fold my typewriter, all wrapped up in an oil-sheet is on one side of the mule and my basket and camp-bed on the other. In the basket is a wash-basin, spare suit, socks . . . books, Bible, papers, rope, passport . . . My 'servant' carries the lantern.

We ride on. As a rule I like to walk for a mile or two to get warmed up in this cold weather, but we start off uphill and my nice Ipswich saddle looks somewhat inviting . . . we go up and up. We were already at 1,500 feet but we climb another 1,000 feet . . . Not a sign of human habitation . . .

I am reading, as I always like to on horseback. This time I am reading the life of C.T. Studd (whom I met in 1906). Do you remember the stir created by the going out to China of The Cambridge Seven? It is a most inspiring life. On I read, chapter after chapter, then turn round and look: oh, what a magnificent view of the mountains towards Tali . . . a huge panorama standing out so clearly in the bright sunshine . . .

By one o'clock everyone is hungry. We turn in to the first house we see and try to get them to cook us a meal. Nothing doing! The women make all kinds of excuses:— have no pots and pans, have no vegetables, have no rice, are busy etc. etc. Finally I go out and see if there is a horse inn in the village, find one and fetch the muleteers with the loads. The woman here is obliging and cooks us a nice meal. While the meal is preparing I sit in the kitchen and chat with the women. I ask them if they have ever heard the gospel. Yes, they have, but they are not Christians . . .

We travel on and on, over the brow of a hill with a full view of the Yungping plain, then down the west side to a small town. Darkness is coming on as your mules clatter over the paved road into the town, but there is moonlight, and oh! the moon is so bright out here. My 'servant' takes me to a smallish inn, but I find the landlord very friendly.

He puts me up in his loft, full of grime, grime, grime. They cook the food just underneath and have no chimneys . . . My head has to avoid one low beam, also the good landlord's bacon, hung up in thick strips on a stick of bamboo across the room. He asks me if I want bacon for my meal, and of course I do, as a change from eggs, but he leaves the rind on — please will he pare the rind off when he makes my breakfast — yes, yes . . . I make the bed — very little to make, for I wrap myself up in a wadded quilt. I have a wash in water from the big pan in the kitchen, undress in the grimy darkness, hang my clothes over a bamboo bin full of beans, turn in and sleep the sleep of the just. Oh your insomniacs of civilised England! let me have them and put them on a mule for thirty miles over our Yunnan mountains, then see what they feel like when their heads touch the pillow at eight o'clock in the evening . . .

A Home in the West

The object of this journey was to meet Roxie and their younger child at Tali, where a gathering of Christian workers was to take place. Roxie was beginning to feel the strain of having no base, and was looking forward to the house James planned for the family in Paoshan. James himself found his correspondence was heavy and he needed time and a place for it to be done adequately. Besides, he enjoyed the company of his children, and now a third child was expected at the end of the year.

Above all, he wanted to settle down to urgent prayer for all the work in the area, and beyond. Roxie was not too well at the time and remembers James's restless sense of burden for prayer. 'I wish Dan was here to pray with!' he exclaimed one day. And soon after, he decided to invite Dan Smith — who was free at the time — to join him in three days of prayer.

James spent as much time in prayer and fasting in these days — the last days of his life — as he had ever done. He had been reading again from John Wesley, and wrote a month before he died:

> I often think that it is only the very, very few who are prepared, by rigorous self-discipline (not a very popular thing nowadays), for a lifetime of great usefulness like John Wesley.

10   BUILT ON ROCK

One Clear Call

The Burma Road winds up from Mandalay over the rocks and lofty scrubland of the border mountains, rising to 11,000 feet and descending on the China side in a series of spectacular hairpin bends. Many years were spent in the building of it, for it was hacked out and laid down virtually by slave labour. However, even the most seasoned traveller is silenced by the grandeur of the terrain it opens up: range upon range of windswept and sun-washed mountains ascending into the clouds. Once it had been completed, in the late 1930s, you could drive from Shanghai to Rangoon by road; it linked the East coast of China with the Bay of Bengal.

The road came straight through Paoshan, and James and Roxie found the little house there became the centre of much coming and going. It was 1938, and people came through now on their way to Kunming, the capital; Muchengpo, the Lisu centre of the south; northwards up the Salween to Luda and beyond; or westwards to Burma itself.

The only way James could get away from the bustle of activity was to find a room for quiet somewhere else. So he found and rented a little attic room opposite the mission house. It was up some dark stairs in the house of an Islamic friend. James put a small table and chair in it, but otherwise it was unfurnished.

There was no window, but he could lift out some
wooden boards to let in light and air.

He would often come here early in the morning,
missing breakfast, to spend some hours in prayer. He
was free here to walk up and down and pray aloud. It
was quiet too, he said, and he could wait and listen for
the will of God both for himself and for the work.
Sometimes at midday there would be a little footstep
on the stair.

'Daddy, mummy says are you coming for a walk
with us?' Almost every day, James, Roxie and the little
fair-haired child walked up to the hills overlooking
Paoshan. James seemed quiet and reflective these days,
Roxie thought, as if he had something on his mind.

'You know, Roxie', he said one day up in the hills,
'even when I've gone, I don't think my work in Yunnan
will be finished.'

She was startled a few days later when he said, 'Mr
Payne is passing through in two weeks' time. I have
some money here for him. If anything happens to me,
you'll know where it is.'

'But I don't understand — '

'I just thought I'd let you know.'

He talked a lot these days about the children's
future and about the baby expected before the end of
the year. It was September already: the event was not
too far off.

On Wednesday, September 21st, James had a
headache. He finished answering some important
letters and then played the little organ for a while
before going to bed. By the next morning his headache
was severe. He sent runners at once to get someone to
be with Roxie.

James had gone down with malignant cerebral
malaria. There was no appropriate medicine in

Paoshan. It was not long before he lost consciousness, and for two days the fever intensified; by Saturday evening he was strangely quiet.

It was a long night for Roxie: James in and out of delirium, the Chinese doctor and nurses hurrying up and down the stairs, the child crying in the darkness. When the sun rose on September 25th 1938, James had gone.

It was a shock to his colleagues. He was only 52 and seemed strong and healthy: they found the news hard to believe.

But for Roxie the whole world was reeling.

Isobel Kuhn wrote to her three days later:

'The very thought of you makes my hand tremble so and the tears come so that I do not know how I can write. The Lisu have just walked in with their unbelievable message . . . Times like this are when we just have to bare our face to the tempest and go on without seeing clearly, without understanding, without any thing but naked faith.'

Some Lisu from the Salween had come down to Paoshan and they carried James's body to the little chapel by the mission house and held a Lisu service for him. Prayers, hymns and tributes were all in Lisu: a token farewell from the thousands of believers scattered over the western ranges.

The Christian funeral that followed a few days later was new to the streets of Paoshan. They filled the chapel with flowers for the service and afterwards a long procession walked through the city carrying silk banners in complete silence. Mr Chao, the tanner, wore white as the chief mourner, or 'son' of the deceased, a courageous thing to do in his own city.

James was buried on a hill overlooking Paoshan, on the lower slopes of the mountains that had been his

home for thirty years. It was a solitary grave among
the pine trees. On the headstone the words were
inscribed in Lisu, in Chinese and in English: 'I am the
Resurrection and the Life: he that believeth in Me,
though he were dead, yet shall he live: and whosoever
liveth and believeth in Me shall never die.'

Isobel Kuhn describes how James's fellow workers
felt — not that they had lost a great leader or
figurehead, but that they had lost a friend.

> After the first shock, there was a desolate feeling, as
> regards human fellowship, that there was no one now
> to work for. 'How Mr Fraser will enjoy hearing about
> this,' was always a first reaction to any joy or bless-
> ing . . . There was no one else on earth who had such a
> complete knowledge of the details of our problems, no
> one who could share so perfectly in our joys and
> sorrows.
>
> And he never disappointed us in the sharing. He
> was more than Superintendent to us, he was our
> missionary ideal, a continual rebuke, challenge and
> stimulus to maintain at any cost the apostolic
> methods of missionary work. His brilliant gifts,
> united with unfailing humility and a sympathy
> motherlike in its tenderness and thoughtfulness, made
> him our refuge at all times of perplexity and need.
> And to win a smile of approval from him was worth
> any extra effort. It is one thing to be praised by a
> person who has no experience of your task; it is quite
> different to win a 'well done' from one who is himself
> a master in that very line of things. We have lost a
> great stimulus, as well as an indispensable counsellor.
> I say 'indispensable', for we still feel that way. Life can
> never be the same to us, without him.

Roxie learned in the weeks that followed that God
brings treasures out of the darkness. At first there was
the almost devastating sense of aloneness, and then the
long journey into Burma for the birth of her third

little girl, accompanied faithfully by a nurse, Dorothy
Burrows. Then there was the long sea journey to
Chefoo to take her second daughter to school. As she
lay in her bunk on the ship, in great weakness, the
baby very ill beside her, Roxie admitted she hardly
wanted to live any longer.

A man came to visit her before she sailed. He was a
Kachin Christian and badly wanted to meet her. Years
before, he said, he had run many miles in murderous
pursuit after James. He had fully intended to kill him,
but James outran him. Some time later he heard the
message of Jesus Christ; he had believed and become
his disciple.

When Roxie reached Chefoo she found Mrs Fitzwilliam, who had also lost her husband in Yunnan.
So they shared a house for the summer — very unlike
the Kachin shanty they had shared before. And Roxie
found Chefoo brimming with life and activity: there
were the sea and the sands, the sports and entertain-
ments, but most therapeutic of all, hundreds of lively
children. 'Everything was planned by a loving Father',
she said later. 'Chefoo was just what I needed.'

Roxie was delayed at the coast for several months
because of the baby's illness and was able to be with
her family when they were taken by the Japanese,
along with the whole CIM school, to the concentration camp at Weihsien. But that is another story.

Lisu Church in Wartime
After James's death, Bible School work among the
tribes continued in strength. The Rainy Season Bible
School became a very fruitful institution. By 1941,
while World War II was at its height, the Bible School
at Luda had ten tribes represented among its students
and 1,000 people present at its graduation ceremony.

Between 1942 and 1943 the Japanese army over-ran Burma and penetrated Lisuland. Missionaries had to escape temporarily, but by 1945 were already coming back to find the tribal churches flourishing.

A Central Church Council was established to encourage fellowship between the various groups of believers. They were already (and had been since their inception) very missionary in outlook, and after an extensive survey by John Kuhn they became aware of scores of separate tribes in the Yunnan mountains who were still unreached.

By 1947 Mr and Mrs Crane and Mr and Mrs Cox had arrived in Lisuland with two loads of Lisu New Testaments. Soon after this a printing press for the tribes arrived in Kunming and was speedily in use. Already a Lisu Gospel magazine was in circulation.

In 1949 the People's Government of China was set up in Peking and the whole of China was under Communism.

The Rainy Season Bible School was held as usual that year, and in 1950 John Kuhn was still travelling with a team of Lisu evangelists and seeing many people put faith in Christ for the first time. There were record attendances at Bible Schools, and in November of that year one hundred people were baptised in Oak Flat Village, bringing the total membership in that area to 1,200, divided among 42 chapels.

The last CIM workers to leave the tribes were John Kuhn and Charles Petersen. As a farewell for them in 1950, 800 Lisu gathered to sing the Hallelujah Chorus; it was a memorable moment — a sacrifice of praise. Missionaries could go back to the comfort of homelands. The Lisu had to stay and face a dark future where they were.

By 1951 the Lisu Church was standing alone without foreign help, thirty years after its birth.

Persecution

During 1951 and the years that followed, the Lisu believers suffered with all the other Christians in China. Little was known about their ordeal until, weary and poverty-stricken, some of them escaped over the mountains to tell the story.

At first worship was forbidden and Bibles and Christian literature confiscated. Then many believers were taken from their families and sent to be re-educated; some were imprisoned. Finally the day came when Christians were put to death for their faith. It was a baptism of fire for a very young church.

The escape of thousands of Lisu into Burma and Thailand is a saga of its own. In his story *Exodus to a Hidden Valley,* Eugene Morse writes one of the most fascinating books of recent years (chosen to be one of the *Readers' Digest* Condensed Books). He tells the story of the trek made by a large group of Christian tribespeople from China over the mountains of Burma and then the setting up of a Christian community in a remote valley.

During the early 1960s, the Cranes, Cookes and Kuhns were in Burma working on the Lisu Old Testament and helping with Bible teaching among the ever-increasing number of tribespeople fleeing from South-west Yunnan. By 1963 they estimated at least 10,000 Lisu had come over to settle in Burma. Adding these to numbers of Christian tribespeople already in Burma, from Putao in the north to the Shan states bordering Thailand in the south, estimates suggested upwards of 60,000 Christians in the tribal churches. Their own leaders had emerged and they led their own Rainy Season Bible Schools.

In 1963 all missionaries had to leave Burma.

The Lisu Bible

The thousands of Lisu Christians now in Burma were waiting month after month for their completed (and revised) Bible. But the authorities would not allow it to enter the country. The Lisu held regular times of prayer for the granting of an import permit.

At last in 1968, a year when there was a mass flight of Christian families from China over the mountains into Burma, the first copies were allowed in. But these few were nowhere near the number needed, and the following years were long years of waiting.

In 1976 missionaries from North Thailand assisted Lisu Christians from Burma in beginning a revision of the whole Bible: a painstaking work which has suffered various setbacks but is still continuing. The first draft has completed the Old Testament and reached Romans in the New, so the great day cannot be far away when the Bible Society will be able to print the revised version of the whole Lisu Bible.

In 1980, however, an earlier edition was produced for the waiting Lisu. 10,000 copies were printed in London and shipped out to Rangoon. For several weeks they were kept at the docks — seven and a half tons of them — until permits were finally granted for their distribution.

Lisu came down from Myitkyina, a journey of 700 miles, bringing presents of honey, fruit and hand-sewn Lisu costumes: an expression of gratitude for the written word of God.

When finally the Bible Society edition is distributed the Lisu church will not only have the complete Bible in its own language, but many thousands of copies of it and more than one version.

A Kingdom which Cannot Fall

Interesting news of the growth and movement of the Lisu and other tribal churches was published in *Asian Outreach* in 1981. Many Lisu, it states, fled to Northern Burma during Communist persecutions and have maintained a strong Christian community there ever since. There are 400 Lisu and Rowang tribal churches in Burma.

During 1981, because of Burmese government relaxation of controls Eugene Morse was able to visit Burma for an intensive preaching and teaching trip. Literature is now being produced to assist 5,000 Lisu leaders in their Bible teaching.

Allyn Cooke is still corresponding with Lisu pastors from his home in California, and sending Bible Commentary booklets to over a hundred of them.

There is a notable move of God among the Naga tribes in Burma, where some thousands have become Christians. These tribes each have their own dialect. Paul Kauffman takes up the story, writing in *Asian Outreach* in 1981:

> They have all decided to learn a common language . . . The language they have reached agreement on is Lisu, a dialect of a large tribal group that fled China after the Communist takeover. There is a strong Christian community among the Lisu. Twenty Nagas have been sent to learn the Lisu language. Fortunately the scriptures, hymnbooks and other Christian literature have been translated into Lisu.
>
> After learning Lisu, the twenty trainees will return to their tribes with a three-fold responsibility: firstly, to teach Lisu to the other Nagas; secondly, to act as

interpreters for Lisu Bible teachers who may minister among the newly-converted Nagas; thirdly, to teach the Word of God to their own people in the Lisu language. We have received an urgent request for Lisu literature for these Naga tribes living in Northern Burma.

But where persecution was unable to destroy the Lisu church — and may even have strengthened it — another insidious attack is being made on their stand for biblical truth. One veteran missionary writes:

I get several letters a week (from Lisu pastors), often one or two a day. The church is being tested by modernistic teachers who are trying to convince them that the Bible is the work of man, the resurrection is a fable and Christ did not rise from the dead; the miracles did not really happen as recorded but are merely illustrative of spiritual truth. But the older teachers are standing for the truth once delivered to the saints, and a growing number of churches are standing with them. Please pray for them that they may not be overwhelmed by the convincing arguments and the pressure brought to bear on them. Some of the pastors have been defrocked and their churches taken away from them.

It is reassuring to read Paul Kauffman's impressions in his survey of this whole theatre of spiritual warfare on the Burma-China borders. News filtering over the mountains from South-west China tells of a strong church still standing where James and his colleagues lived out their lives years ago. Kauffman writes:

God is moving also among the tribal Christians of South-west China. Since the relaxation inside China over 70 tribal congregations have come out in the open. One of these tribal congregations numbers 5,000 people. In this area along the old Burma road, north-ward to the Tibetan border there is strong Christian activity. At Christmas time over 2,000 tribal people attended a Bible Conference. Chinese officials were amazed, in fact bewildered. They stood on the platform of the convention and asked how many in the crowd were Christians. All but two stood to their feet in open testimony. Those present said that the local authorities then assured the Christians that they had no reason to fear, and even offered to help them establish Three-Self churches.

Standing back and looking at the development throughout that entire region, one can clearly see the hand of God, not only upon His own people, but reaching out to those who do not know Him.

When God Himself sets up His kingdom, the gates of hell shall not prevail against it.

North Thailand Advance

In the early 1950s, missionaries from the Overseas Missionary Fellowship (the new name for the China Inland Mission) made a survey of the mountains of North Thailand. As the map will show you, this area lies up against Burma and is not far from the borders of China. The mountain people here are tribesfolk very similar to those of South-West China. At least 250,000 tribespeople were found to be living in the 42,000 miles covered by the survey.

Here again there were Lisu. But there were also Yao, Akha, Karen, Lahu and Meo (now called Hmong). Veterans from China were joined by new workers in bringing the message of Jesus Christ to these people. Isobel Kuhn's *Ascent to the Tribes* gives a realistic insight into all that this involved. These mountain missionaries had to face all the physical hardships and spiritual battles that had been faced on the Salween ranges — and they still do.

Let me show you, said an onlooker after a visit to

North Thailand, a couple of single girls living in a tiny wooden house, sleeping virtually on planks of wood, and fetching water from a spring half a mile down the mountain, praying and waiting for any sign of spiritual interest from the villagers, and I will show you a little of what it means to be a corn of wheat falling into the ground to die.

Lives have been laid down by missionaries in Thailand just as they were in China, for the sake of Jesus Christ. Little churches have been established. A full account of the work now going on is given in *Dawn Wind:* a fascinating story of the varied tribal response as well as OMF's other work in Thailand. This book also outlines the rapid social changes evident now that modern medicine, agriculture, education and radio are reaching these hitherto inaccessible regions.

There is the continual reminder as Thailand looks at her eastern neighbours, and plays host to their thousands of refugees, that political skies are cloudy: days of freedom to preach salvation through Christ alone may be numbered. The vast majority of Thailand's population has never heard that there is no other Name under heaven given among men whereby we must be saved.

Posthumous Award

In 1979 an interesting document arrived in England. It measures about ten inches by seven and is the colour of pale parchment. It came from the leaders of the Lisu church at Lashio, on the Burmese side of the border mountains.

On December 23rd, 1978, they had planned an anniversary to commemorate two things: firstly, the founding of their Lashio church ten years before;

secondly, the founding of their church in Lisuland in 1920.

They knew Allyn Cooke, of course, and sent him a similar certificate of honour to mark their gratitude for a lifetime spent for God among them. But was he the very first to come to their village in China? they asked.

Allyn's mind went back over the years. He saw again the lonely figure on the mountains of the Cold Country, bringing a message year after year that nobody wanted to hear.

No, Allyn wrote back, he was not the very first. And he told them about James. Ah yes, they said, their parents had known Elder Brother Number Three. They would like to send a certificate of honour posthumously for the man who had first brought them the message of eternal life.

The certificate is written in Lisu, and translates:

> From the time of the establishment of the Lisu Church in the Shan States, Kokong County, Six Families District, Muddy Pool Village in 1920 until December 23rd 1978 there are 58 years. Within that period, Rev. J O Fraser, Elder Brother Number Three, since you served willingly and warmheartedly, doing the work of the church of Jesus Christ in obedience to the command of God, the leaders of the church present you with this certificate of honour.
> Date: 1978, 12th month, 26th day.
> Place: Lashio, New Village, Burma.

James was only one of hundreds involved in establishing the church in this area of the world. His contribution to ideas of missionary strategy and principle was clearly a valuable one. But his richest legacy was in his understanding of how God works at any time, in any place, through any person.

There was no avoiding the cost here. It was costly at the beginning of James's service and went on being costly to the end. It seems there is no other way to know the full blessing of God. To the disciple of Jesus Christ it is perhaps surprising that anyone should expect otherwise. There was something of rebuke in King David's voice when he turned to Araunah in 2 Samuel 24.24. 'I will not offer . . . to the Lord my God that which costs me nothing.'